January Fourth

I called the veterin.   ~uld

drop off Pietra very early in the morning at his office. Her hyperthyroidism

seemed to be getting the best of her despite all the attempts at drugs and

diet.

At around 9 p.m. she tiptoed downstairs to the laundry room, as she

always did, to where her litter box was located. We were alone in the house

and the Boston Celtics was playing, that very single television event that

makes me press the "on" button and slumber in front of the screen, despite

of the appalling amount of money we are charged for cable. It took me a

while to realize that Pietra did not come back up to be around me as usual.

I soon found her sleeping next to her box over a pile of dirty clothes. I

picked her up, although she always hated to be held, and strangely, she

never felt so light. As if somehow she had lost much of her weight in that

brief passage of time, too short for such a mass to disappear from her body.

I carried upstairs this resigned feline who at last gave in to be embraced by

me.

I placed Pietra in her bed and gave her some water. She reluctantly

nibbled on some food, and I mindlessly returned to my role of 21st century self-centered, sports-watching troglodyte ... uncertain of my actions, but hoping she would be ok.

I thought about it. I could just rush out the door and look for an animal emergency service. But I didn't. I wanted her to be alright at that moment. And I rationalized - favoring doing nothing - that since I would be taking her to the animal hospital the very first thing in the morning, I could just as well have another beer and go back to my brainless activity. Sickness brings out a peculiar trait in me. It always did. I sink my head in the sand.

But it took me only a glance from a few feet away as I got up and walked by her bed to realize that I had lost the closest thing I ever had from having a child.

I can't imagine that I loved Pietra any less.

And so, the goal was cemented in my mind from the inception. I intend to cross the country on my bicycle and record the story of this ride, even if not much of a story will come out of it. I will be riding by myself. Judging places and encounters; likely making gross assumptions; saying things that would not occur to anybody else. As Nietzsche said "you never access reality independent of your beliefs."

But I will try to convey my description as honestly as I can. Most importantly, the account of my preparations for this bicycle trip should begin six months before my departure - today, the fourth of January, 2017 - exactly a year after the loss of that beautiful furry creature that shared a most cherished slice of time with me on this planet. It's also the same day that I launch my fundraising for The Merrimack River Feline Rescue Society.

End of January

With little more than four months to go before I fly from Massachusetts to Oregon where I intend to begin my ride, I'm painfully biding my time, especially as the New England winter rolls in, not too ominously so far I must say. But the snow is out there and thinking of training is out of the question. So I'm face-lifting my bicycle and amassing the items I will need as I plan to spend the whole summer riding back to Newburyport.

Got new wheels with extra spokes for strength; stronger and wider fork that allows me to install a front rack and fenders, along with new pedals, crankset and cassette. I've been poking around Amazon for quite some time to equip myself with every item that I might (or might not!) need. Items such as a discontinued digital camera from Sony that requires a special kind of memory stick that always comes with limited amount of data space and that you can only find in the dark bowels of online shopping! A Bluetooth folding keyboard to connect with my phone so I can do my stellar writing on the road; a somewhat light backpacking hammer to pound tent pegs into the ground and dig drainage trenches; solar power charger for my phone, Bluetooth speaker attached to the handlebar, and a couple of mp3 players loaded with music and books on tape; also, waterproof bicycle shoe-covers, waterproof pants, jacket and poncho, and panniers. At some point I might give an account of every single item I will be carrying with me, for the benefit of human wisdom. Which, last time I counted neared eighty.

I must say that although my excitement toward this ride is very high, I honestly don't see it by any means as the approaching of a major feat. Granted, I will certainly struggle mightily in the throes of a nasty hill, or worse, a series of hills where the weight of four panniers makes you wanna get off and walk all the way home. But, aside from the logistics of finding the time, I strongly believe a cross-country ride to be under most people's capabilities.

You sit on your bicycle and rotate the pedals as slow as you want, ad infinitum, for as long as you wish before you find a place to eat and drink like a starving hyena; climb back on and do it all over for a few more hours;

repeat the hungry-hyena role again then set up tent or rent a motel room just to start again next day.

Barring any personal misgivings one may have about spending that much time on the road, or the fear of traffic, bears and other earthlings, the whole thing is very much within reach of anyone with the minimum necessary conditions.

Then again, I'm saying this long before I'm actually riding! Furthermore, because the idea of writing about it, or indeed, having someone else spending time reading it, feels quite narcissistic at times. Nevertheless, having traveled for six months around the States a few years ago without keeping a journal about the unusual and surreal encounters I had, I don't want to repeat the same mistake.

End of February

School vacation week is upon us and the snow is packing a bruising punch on New England. It's useless to even think about riding or training (I refuse to use indoor trainers), so the second best option is to finally get a grip on learning some bicycle maintenance. Thanks to my friend Brendan, a former bicycle racer and currently I master swimmer on the team I coach, I now feel a bit less anxious about mechanical issues that can go wrong during a long ride. Brendan and I recently spent a few hours in my basement deconstructing a couple of bicycles - and possibly our livers - meticulously tasting new brewings and going over tools, parts and knowledge that I must acquire. I learned quite a bit, but essentially, I learned to recognize my cluelessness toward this piece of machine that I'm so fond of and which I should have had deeper familiarity with its basic functioning long before. But I just don't have a mechanical type of mind.

First Day of Spring

Thirty-three degrees in Massachusetts of course. I'm a few steps away from having it all set to begin my ride. Bought the front rack and a Pedro's ICM multi-tool, leaving pretty much only a pair of fenders and an extra tire left to be purchased. With *snow days* season almost over I can now set the date for my flight to Portland, Oregon. We had four snow days so far which pushes the end of school year to June 22, and my departure to Friday, June 23. Assuming I begin riding on June 24 from the coast of Oregon, I'm left with 15 days to ride one thousand miles to Bozeman, Montana, for a four day rest and a visit to Yellowstone Park. Fifteen days, a thousand miles, average of 66.66666666 miles per day barring any day off! Ugh! The 66 miles a day isn't so bad. The fifteen days without a rest sounds a bit like a "pain in the ass."

I signed up to Twitter against all my organic rejection of social media. Unfortunately I have to adjust to the times. I announced to all my physical education students - more than 400 of them - that I'm biking across the country this summer and I want them to follow my trip and, just maybe, be inspired to have an active summer.

Sixty degrees. Finally!

Or so they say. Tomorrow. Sunday, April 9. It looks like the official start of bicycle riding season in New England. I've got to get my first 50-mile to prepare my head and bones. Any attempt to train for my ride has been hampered by an incredible sequence of dreary days so far. But tomorrow, I will bring myself up to speed!

What's not doing so well either is my fund-raising. Then again, I absolutely despise to ask others for money. What a complex psychological exchange the donation of money embodies. The multiplicity of feelings involved in receiving and giving money is hard to distill. And the best one can do - and I think is what we often end up doing - is to simply ignore them all, take the money and run (in case you're receiving it) or to dish out the money and pretend you're not pumping yourself up with a little jolt of internal superiority. Of course, this is a crude summary of that exchange. It also unearths feelings of gratitude, joy, shame, adulation, submission, paternalism, exploitation, mistrust and admiration.

What I know is that I don't like to be involved in either side of that exchange, and now I find myself even going to local newspapers to publicize my ride and campaign.

One Month to Go

Exactly one month away to begin this ride. Anybody reading this (anybody reading this?) must be thinking, "Enough already. Could you just leave now please?"

The pile of stuff I will be carrying keeps getting bigger. It's nagging me. As I write, right now, I remember I haven't added a piece a soap yet! Should I?

My bicycle is pretty much ready. I added a backlight that can be seen from two kilometers, day and night. It flashes like a cruiser's light and it will either alert drivers away from me or annoy the hell out of them all making them want to crush the damn light along with the rider! Also purchased two Gatorskin Continental anti-puncture tires, an old-fashion handlebar mirror that sticks out to the left of the bicycle to check out oncoming cars, handlebar phone holder, fenders, front rack, first-aid kit, and a whole box of Gutsey's Boston "wicked strong bah" energy bars. What else do I need?

Time to fly

Time to wake up at 3 a.m., hop on the bus to the airport in Boston and finally fly to Portland, Oregon.

Six hours later I'm staring down at the mountains of Idaho and eastern Oregon, including Mount Helen, Mount Hood and a whole lot of other tall mountains down there that I will not long be battling through the power of a crankset. My friend Brendan picked me up at the airport to drive me to his sister's house from where I would begin my journey.

Thanks to Brendan my trip didn't begin as a total rookie disaster. *Failing to plan is planning to fail* said a great swimming coach who I can't name right now. Brendan is too polite to express his real feelings about the whole thing but ever since I mentioned that I would be riding across the country I could see the concern on his face for my lack of realistic preparations for the crucial first day.

Where is your bicycle going to be shipped to? Who is going to put it together to make sure it is ready when you get there? How will you get to the coast of Oregon which is 100 miles from Portland? Where would you sleep on the first night?

I could almost see his brain cells spinning in puzzlement each time my answers to those questions were wholly unconvincing. Brendan planned it all out. He flew the day before to Portland, began to put my bicycle back together - after already being the one who showed me how to break it down for shipping ten days earlier - got me accommodations at his sister's house and on top of it all gave me a nice tour of an interesting section of Portland with lots of vibrant bars, breweries, cafes and overall just cool-looking people walking around. How do I even begin to thank him for all that?

Brendan's sister, Aubrey, is married to Tim a serious cyclist and family physician. Tim, just like Brendan, knows everything that should be known about bicycles and their functioning, best parts, etc. Needless to say, I could also see the worry and incredulity on his face regarding the appropriateness of my bicycle to the upcoming task. Altogether, bike and bags weighted about 70 pounds - or more - an older bicycle mind you.

Dipping the Wrong Wheel

Ride No. 1 = Fort Stevens, Coast of Oregon, to Portland, Oregon, 106.1 miles

The morning of June 24 finally materialized as Brendan's friend from Portland, a mighty friendly, self-proclaimed handsome guy named Aaron arrived at 5:30 in the morning to drive us over 100 miles to the Pacific coast so I could dip my wheel - more on that later - in the ocean, take the required picture, and pedal back to Newburyport, my sweet home.

Brendan and I getting ready for ride number 1.

As we drive down toward the coast through Route 30, the magnitude of the task I had set for myself and Brendan becomes dreadfully clear.

One-hundred and six miles on the first day which happened to feature ... 104 degrees half way through our ride.

Aaron dropped us off at Fort Stevens, we gave him a big hug for the ride which it was all he would accept for his great favor, then Aaron handed me this iron bar that supposedly only law enforcement personnel can have, which you sort of snap it forward making it expand three times becoming a great tool for protection against chasing dogs and sapiens alike.

The first 10 miles was a breeze. Judging by the ease and nimbleness of that beginning I felt like the whole ride would be just dandy... until the heat began to get the best of us. I didn't have my saddlebags. I didn't need them, and yet, my bicycle itself weighted about 30 pounds, almost twice as much as Brendan's bicycle, and he is 10 years younger and used to belong to a bicycle racing team in China!

Route 30 runs all the way back to Portland, from Astoria. It is a major access route and the traffic is intense. The type of road that cyclists shouldn't be on. Shoulders are non-existent in many spots, most notably during a long and painful ascent, about 50 miles into our trip. We had to stop several times for shade and cold drinks as the temperature kept getting higher, the more tired we became, eventually reaching the promised land of 104 degrees.

Brendan got a second wind in the last third of our ride when I, for one, began to fade... and fade I did. All the way to the last two miles when a bend around the block to arrive at his sister's house felt like an eternity. With sore buttocks and risking sun stroke right off the bat, my long trip started with the longest mileage I would be facing for several days. It was fun though. It was a blast to ride with Brendan and share so many fragments of memory that are attached to long road trips, such as that red truck that almost took our skin sample, the beautiful landscape of eastern Oregon, the young kid that rocketed by us without saying hello just to bonk a few miles later facing the humiliation of being overtaken three times even after Brendan and I stopped to cool off. The amazing blue eyes of the girl who gave us free drinks at a coffee stand, most likely pitying our sore state is also engraved in my memory.

The New England spring didn't allow me to prepare as much as I should for such a grand start. But the help of a generous friend and his family in Portland made it all possible. It got me on the right footing.

About that "dipping the wrong wheel." Talk about a screw-up. Brendan flies across the country to help me out. His friend drives 100 miles to drops us off at the Pacific Ocean just so I can dip the wheel in it ... and I get the wrong one in! So I have a lovely picture of myself facing the ocean, dipping the front wheel, as if I'm riding all the way to Africa ... or backwards to Massachusetts!

Me, mindlessly dipping the wrong wheel into the Pacific!

And So it Goes

Ride No. 2 = Portland to Cascade Rocks, Oregon, 57 miles

Next morning I loaded my bicycle for the first time with all four saddlebags, which from then on would be a feature of my life, plus my small cooler on top of the front rack. After saying goodbye to Brendan's sister Aubrey, I followed Tim and Brendan out of Portland and into the bicycle path along the Columbia River for my first taste of this river which would be my companion for many days.

But before I get that far, a note about biking through and out of Portland. In a word: *Paint!*

That's all it takes. Portland makes a concerted effort to be truly bicycle friendly, and yet, pretty much all it takes is a consistent demarcation of bicycle lanes with strong road painting. Certain sections are divided with other features but the sense that one gets from crossing through the whole city is that any other town could, if they cared to, do just as well. Any place could be as bicycle friendly. Any city could have hundreds of people on their bicycles like we see in Portland. It just takes dedication, leadership, and .... Paint! Do you hear me Boston? Newburyport?

We cruised through the city feeling safe and respected, sharing the road with dozens of young and old on their bicycles, looking happy and relaxed. Human society can work sometimes!

Brendan and Tim accompanied me all the way to the historical Route 30. We hugged, and right then and there the reality of spending the next two months alone on the road hit me. I felt ok … I had done a solo road trip before, but not as audacious.

The made-up word "humbition" comes to mind (via the outstanding podcasts series by the philosophy professor Wes Cecil). The extent of the task ahead of me felt almost too brutal and *humbling* to contemplate at that moment, and yet, I experienced a palpable sense of relief inside my chest as my legs pressed on the crankset and the *ambition* to just go forward never wavered.

And so I pedaled. Faced a long ascent of a few miles putting to the test my capacity to go uphill for the first time with all my gear.

My stop for the night was Cascade Locks Campground, 57 miles later. I went through a long stretch of touristic ups and downs on Route 30 with its famous falls and depressing lines of cars with stifled tourists exiting them just to walk to the closest snack stand and bathroom, take some pictures, and jump right back into their cars. I must have passed them all as

I cruised by a few traffic jams. Then again, they certainly passed me later on, looking out the window at this lone goofy cyclist wearing his Grateful Dead bicycle jersey, struggling to climb the hills, and they probably felt happy not to be me.

View from Historic Route 30 in Oregon, along the Columbia River.

But before I got to my destination, a very peculiar event took place along the trail that runs parallel to Highway 84.

I must preface by expressing my unmovable non-belief in anything supernatural. But if ever I were to find my "guardian angel" - the concept itself puzzles me - this was a fitting example. Out of nowhere in this trail you find a spot where you have to walk down several sets of 10 steps toward the next level of the trail. Quite unusual for a "bicycle trail" if I can assume that it was built as one.

At this point, my bicycle - aka: "Scarlet" (it's red after all and it's named after one of my favorite Dead songs "Scarlet Begonias") - weighted 28 pounds by itself along with what I calculate to be between 40 and 45 pounds of gear. So, to lift my bicycle up and walk all those steps I would have to carry 70 pounds of awkward load. Just as I'm arriving at that spot an older gentleman appears out of nowhere reaching the very top of the stairs. I had just cycled for hours without finding one single individual at the trail.

He had this handsome face that 70-year-old people in peace with their past and present seem to acquire; with bright grey hair and a gentle expression. He looks at me just as I am about to begin lugging my bicycle down the steps and say:

"I have to watch."

I look at him trying not to convey any idea that I expect him to help me, but I am a bit puzzled with his comment.

"You have to watch?" I reply.

He turns to me with a serious expression on his face as if telling me that naturally, that is his job, then says resolutely:

"Yes."

He did watch me going down the first two sets of steps, slowly and carefully, actually feeling my shoulder muscles tighten in each step. After succeeding half way I look up and see him slowly walking away as if we never met. Surely a very gentle human being.

That night I made it into Cascade Locks Campground. Paid the five dollars self-service fee, found a nice spot to set up my Eureka Solitaire little tent facing the river and felt that my trip was definitely under way.

You never fail to encounter interesting individuals when traveling slowly on a bicycle ... As soon as I began to get settled a young man stopped by to give me a rundown of the camp. He commented on my bicycle jersey with a big "Steal Your Face" Grateful Dead design and immediately set out to talk about concerts, pot stories, and his life after the wild years. He gave me the code for the showers (1598 if you ever stop there and the office is closed) and promised to provide me with a joint should I need one.

I know I look the part, with my long hair, peace signs, Dead shirts and patches, and my absolute devotion to GD compositions and Jerry Garcia's musicianship, but that's where I draw the line. I'm the "square" Dead Head type. Granted, you've got to see me free-dancing through a Dead's concert!

Cascade Locks Campground. First camping night. My Scarlet getting some rest.

Cascade Locks is a beautiful spot. That weekend, across from the campground, a "Daniel Boone" gathering was taking place. I kid you not!

At night I shared a couple of porter pints with my tent neighbor, Lori, a traveling nurse who spends about six months in one location then is placed somewhere else where she is needed. Lori had the sad look of someone who's not found a nest. She is an avid hiker, which brought her camping at Cascade Locks. We had a sort of uptight conversation, until by chance I mentioned my love of basketball. Her eyes lit up. Lori used to be a basketball player, and professed to have a love/hate relationship with it, but her mood changed as she described her passion for Larry Bird and the Celtics ... Just like me. We said goodnight after a nice chat and I slept in my tent for the first time on this trip. Tried to! Small tents, thin backpacking mattresses, and plastic pillows require a serious training in order for you to have a restful night.

The Birth of the Wind

Ride No. 3 = Cascade Locks, Oregon, to Horsethief Campground, Washington, 54.5 miles

The weather changed dramatically overnight at Cascade Locks. A strong wind began to pound on our tents. Little did I know that despite a few tribulations and almost being blown away the following night, that westerly wind on my back would be my best friend for days to come.

Next morning with a strong tailwind I jumped on Highway 84 again, this time planning to cross the Columbia River after the Town of Hood River onto the more scenic and calmer Route 12 East in Washington State.

The wind picked up to great intensity during the day, and by the time I had to walk across the bridge onto Route 12, wind gusts were measured between 50 and 60 miles an hour. With my heavy bicycle, a steady stream of trucks, and my not-so-walking-friendly bicycle shoes, I had a tremendously hard time crossing the bridge. I had to walk for another half mile beyond the bridge until my bicycle faced east again and I could actually ride without being blown off the road. To give it a sense of how bad it was, mid-way through the bridge I met this girl, holding on to the bridge rail not able to go anywhere. She looked at me through a mesh of blowing hair and said: "With a bike it would be easier." Well, not really. I was risking being pushed under any incoming vehicle, couldn't keep my balance, couldn't ride, and on top of that had to push a heavy bicycle across the bridge.

Heading east, my bicycle was moving well, but Route 12 is full of ups and downs and winding curves often forcing me to battle side gusts, and making my way forward too dangerous to keep on. I had to put an end to today's ride as soon as possible.

Not far ahead, I saw a sign for the Horsethief State Park going down a steep hill. I jumped on the only possibility that I could envision at that moment to get out of the wind. I rode down the hill leading to the park, conscious that if I couldn't find anything down there I would be in big trouble going back up against the wind, already exhausted, and not knowing where else to find shelter that day.

That area of Washington State, along the Columbia River is absolutely devoid of vegetation, barring some oasis of trees here and there. Down the hill, I found a small campground surrounded by all kinds of tall trees that looked like they could be toppled by the wind at any moment. But I encountered a smiley John and his lovely wife who showed me around the camp offering different options to spend the night. I took a sort of teepee/cabin covered with canvas that flapped like the world was going to fly into the heavens all night long. But to my amazement that thing held up through the night and by morning the winds were manageable enough to ride uphill, hop on Route 12 again and head east.

Horse Thief Campground. Seen from Route 12, Washington State.

Truck Stop Pasta Alfredo

Ride No. 4 = Horsethief to Boardman, Oregon, 81.9 miles

An unexpected feature of southern Washington State along Route 12 given its general bareness, is the large number of wineries. And they are quite fancy indeed. Stopping at one along the way that morning, I was surprised to find a lovely Mediterranean-style patio next to a cliff overlooking the river. The patio featured bright green hanging vines, classy tables and chairs, and a large mural advertising recent and upcoming concerts taking place at their location. The likes of Gogo Dolls, Steve Winwood, Santana and ZZ Top. Who knew! Being still early in the morning the tasting room wasn't yet open, but they filled me up with fresh cold water. Regretfully I didn't get to taste the wine.

Somewhere around 20 miles past the winery, and having failed to find any other source of water or food along the way, I ran into a major junction where the crossing road led to a bridge about two miles down a steep hill and back into Oregon, again going over the Columbia River. A sign on Route 12 at that junction warned me "83 miles before the next service station." Which meant that I would most likely not find any food or water for that many miles staying on Route 12. I didn't want to be low on water and was feeling a bit weak for lack of breakfast. Searching on my phone, it showed me a truck stop across the river, and the "world famous" Linda's Restaurant attached to it. It sounded promising, but before getting there I would have to cross back over the Columbia River, after all my struggles to make it to this side of the river yesterday.

Stopping at a farm stand right before the bridge I was told that no one ever crosses the bridge on a bicycle, and that there wasn't even room to walk across, never mind cycling. Looking at the bridge I noticed that trucks and cars ran just a few inches from the guardrail on either side and I knew that they would not be happy to see a cyclist blocking their way all across. The prognosis wasn't very good. The chances of getting squashed by a truck looked way too real. So I hung around the farm stand for a while hoping to hitch a ride with a pick-up truck or the like. Nothing came of it, and anyhow, I hate to bother strangers.

I evaluated all my choices. I could, a. Ride across and most likely be run over; b. Go back up to Route 12, taking that big long hill all the way to the top and ride all the 83 miles without much food; c. I could load up on fruits and water at this farm stand then go back up to Route 12; or d. Which I embraced, I could walk my bicycle across the bridge squishing myself against the guardrail with each approaching car or truck. I knew that once I hit Linda's Restaurant I would not come back over the bridge. I would simply stay on Highway 84 in Oregon again, going straight east over a mostly flat terrain. A lot of traffic, but the rewards in terms of miles accomplished would be tremendous.

So, to everyone's surprise at the farm stand who by now knew of my dilemma, I began to push my bicycle against the upcoming traffic over the bridge, pulling it tight against my body and the guardrail every time something came toward me.

Most truckers didn't look upset at me for giving them the extra challenge of trying not to kill me. Often they would wave or give me a thumbs up noticing my effort to give them as much space as possible when they approached. That was a long and labored crossing for sure.

But I made it. Went straight to Linda's to look for something I could eat. How do you find a vegetarian choice at a truck stop in the middle of nowhere? Pasta Alfredo. Bingo! Just five minutes later I was bestowed a watery, tasteless, utterly disgusting spaghetti alfredo with deep fried oily garlic bread on the side. And I kindly smiled twice to the waitress when she inquired about my food! I hate to complain, plus it's not their fault I don't eat the house's specialties like bacon, beef, fried chicken, etc., right?

I couldn't finish that damn Pasta Alfredo for the life of me despite being so hungry. Grabbed some junk snacks at the gas station, stocked up on water and drinks, then rode 60 miles non-stop all the way to the town of Boardman and its very neat campground right off Highway 84.

Highway 84 by the Columbia River in Oregon

The young girl at the campground office told me there was no room for tents on weekdays but I could take an RV space and set up my tent on gravel because every morning at 6 a.m., the sprinklers would come on throughout the camp and I would never be able to know where they're hidden below the grass. I took my chances and set up the tent on a piece of grass next to the gravel.

After pitching my tent I walked about ten to fifteen minutes toward the main junction in town, sat a at local somewhat friendly joint, ordered food and a pint and after breaking into a conversation with the older lady behind the counter, I was told the beer was on the house and she wished me luck on my trip.

Note to self: never fail to tell bartenders about your trip.

Six a.m. came and went and all was well and dry around my tent.

Citizens of Walla Walla!

Ride No. 5 = Boardman, Oregon, to Walla Walla, Washington, 82.3 miles

I started my ride a bit late this morning, something that would happen repeatedly throughout my trip. I like to unwrap the morning slowly. I wonder if people are generally nicer in the morning. Or maybe we're all too cranky to have any sort of interaction, good or bad, early in the morning. Perhaps we just leave each other alone more often at this time.

I hopped on Highway 84 again. The traffic was intense but the tailwind gave me a boost for my entire ride. I was flying along the Columbia River for the entire day, blasting all my bicycle lights and stopping wherever I could to find water.

By the time I reached the exit ramp from the highway into Walla Walla, Washington, I could barely push myself forward. Little did I know the trials that awaited me in a few days though. Today I took up my first motel room of the ride. Felt guilty, but I was soon confronted with the reality that I couldn't just find campgrounds everywhere I went.

How can you not fall in love with a place when one of the first people you see is a guy driving out of a parking lot in front of you, donning a full Batman costume, and yelling to everyone around: "I salute you citizens of

Walla Walla," without any hint of mockery or jest? You couldn't help but take him seriously and wave back. The scene was so surreal you couldn't react accordingly.

I kept walking downtown and found a nice live music venue with very good musicians playing groovy songs. I sat at the bar to order some food and engaged in a conversation with a guy named Ron next to me. What are the odds?

Soon the owner found out what I was doing, and although he was an older guy he sounded like an avid cyclist and pulled me to his table to talk all things bicycle and the routes I should follow the next day. The tricky part though, is that the music was so good, and a bit on the loud side so I kept smiling like an idiot without hearing him and he kept talking non-stop. At some point I must have agreed to ride together the next day, because half way through next day's ride I got a call from him asking over my whereabouts!

Next morning I went back downtown and found a cool breakfast place with lots of veggie and healthy choices that you only find at places with a certain vibe. Grabbed two large iced coffees at Starbucks and waited until eleven a.m. for The Cyclery, where a great guy named Michael changed my chain and replaced my shoe cleats given that I had destroyed them by walking back and forth over the Columbia River upon all kinds of debris and lose gravel. Got their last pair of cleat-covers too so now I can do my walking-in-between-cycling without ruining another pair of cleats and ending up having to ride with sandals.

I had a hard time finding the route out of the city as recommended by the people at the bicycle shop, and when I did began to ride on, it became obvious that it was a great route for a weekend cyclist without four saddlebags on his bicycle. In fact, from Walla Walla to Dayton, Washington, I began to experience the climbing that was to come for the next several days.

At some point on my ride I ran into this lady sitting at the roadside talking to a driver - another Ron, mind you - and I found out that she was crossing the country on foot. Her name was Barbara. She had some sort of spiritual reason in mind, which I didn't get, but, regardless, she was pulling a wheeled cart attached to her hips and had left the Atlantic Coast many months ago. I was happy for her that she would, soon(ish) make her way to California, the final destination. Despite being very short on cash as she told me, she offered me a bag of fresh berries that someone handed to her that day. I declined, grabbed a couple, which were unbelievably delicious and said goodbye, totally in awe.

Let There Be a Lazy Day

Ride No. 6 =Walla Walla to Dayton, Washington, 29.2 miles

It's still too early into my cross-country and I'll forgive myself for misjudging my body's ability to put on more work day after day. Did only 30 miles today, mostly due to the scarcity of options to spend the night further on.

After a quick stop at a little town called Waitsburg, which seemed to have retained much of the charm of old towns along with a modern functionality, I entered the town of Dayton, Washington, and couldn't help to notice a big billboard at the entrance of town saying something along these lines: "Big media, stop lying to us. Fake News" and of course President Trump's name somewhere in there.

It's good to know where a town stands when you're entering it right! Not that I would ever discuss politics with anyone along this ride *When travelling, always espouse the ideology of your host,* is my mantra.

But that big ideological in-your-face made me think. Of course it sort of pricks your buttocks a bit. I don't share Trump's views of the world. In fact it's impossible to make sense of his convictions aside from a *smash and burn* approach to most issues that confront him.

Regardless, that billboard left a bad taste in my mouth. And it's not just because I could never vote for someone like Trump, but it reminded me of the utter impossibility of having a candid, honest, intelligent discussion with pretty much anyone who does not share your views in this country without immediately turning into ad-hominem attacks. Criticize ideas, opinions, assumptions, not the people who manifest them! Shouldn't be so excruciatingly hard to eliminate the "you're an idiot" and put in its place "I completely disagree with you, and this is why..." And follow this path ad infinitum if necessary, but always on the basis of mutual respect.

A few years ago I was reading a piece from an American philosopher who I couldn't name right now, and in a brief passage he talked about the idea of searching for what's *intrinsically right*. That passage never left my head. I built a whole version of the perfection of human society based on that ... in my mind of course! But honestly, I thought a lot about it. I still do. I looked up the word "intrinsic," and it said: *belonging to a thing by its very nature*. Does my statement - any statement - about the president belong to the thing by its very nature? I don't know. I might be bluffing. Let's take a look. Let's see if we can find what's intrinsically right about the views and beliefs we hold. And the way we'll do it is by taking away the "me against you" character of our arguments these days and substitute for "us against the problem." I can assume that Trump is wrong when he says that CNN and others are fake news media, but unless we look at it with the ultimate goal of peeling all the unfounded layers of mere opinions and trying to get to what's *intrinsically right* regarding his statement, we are continually stuck in Neverland. A land full of shouting, offenses, misconceptions, fear and hatred for each other.

Intrinsically right, the point at which I can't deny the rock-bottom reality, and truth, I'm faced with. We might never get to that point. The problem of "ultimate truth" is a long and complicated one in philosophy. Whole careers have been built on the study and teaching of epistemology (how do we know what we know?) It doesn't really matter what we call it. Ultimate truths may not even exist to begin with, but the process is the *Tao* - the way!

What a way to move human society further would that be! A society where I'm free to blurt out any sort of argument and opinion I want, but I'm also responsible for making sure that my statement reflects and belongs to the very nature of the issue. To the *thing in itself*. And I'm also conscious of others' rights to contest, so I'm open to argue my point. Not to shoot you 'cuz you don't agree with me!

I'm asking too much right? Of course I'm willingly displaying a gross naiveté. Human relations are too messy. Humans are too flawed for sure. We don't generally get along that well ... we often appear to simply put up with one another's existence in this planet, because we have to. One of Freud's three human miseries - the existence of the *other*.

We'll not survive this way. It's going to take a lot of serious look into the aims of naive objectives to make real changes in how society functions so we can actually call ourselves *developed* and *civilized*. So long as we keep rolling the ball along and gathering more dirt as it goes, expecting that somehow things will clean themselves up, it won't happen. We'll destroy ourselves before that.

Just as I would be looking for my own destruction had I taken anyone up on the reason and veracity of the statement displayed on the welcome billboard.

I took up a motel room, went to a lovely Mexican restaurant next door and sat down for hours to write. I never said anything slightly political ... I hope!

Crazy Ron at Hell's Gate

Ride No. 7 = Dayton, Washington, to Lewiston, Idaho, 74.4 miles

I left Dayton with a miserly egg and cheese muffin at a gas station then rode through Pomeroy, a small, sweet town where I had a candid chat at a coffee/hardware store - yes, go figure - then sat down outside to enjoy my iced coffee just as a friendly 16-year-old boy comes up to me and starts telling me everything about the town. It was so inspiring to hear him share his knowledge of the place with me. He took a picture of me sitting in front of the store, and after saying goodbye; he walked about 10 yards away, turned around and said:

"By the way, I love your shirt."

"Really, do you know the Grateful Dead?" I ask.

"Sure! I've been listening since I was a kid."

One cool dude indeed.

Just chilling in Pomeroy, Washington State.

Funny how some places just immediately seem to exhale negative vibes (granted, all experiences are personal) but Lewiston, Idaho, my destination for the day, was the first place in which in a matter of minutes I had two cars going by with their young and boisterous drivers yelling expletives at me. Apparently I was "supposed" to ride only on the sidewalks according to a "friendly suggestion" of the driver. From the second car, the driver and passenger simply seemed to enjoy cursing at cyclists. A great hobby indeed!

Found a nice vibe at a Starbucks store though, where my gift cards from my students and swimmers always come handy. It was hot, really hot, and a couple of iced coffees later I headed to Hell's Gate Campground, a few miles out of town.

Entering the campground I was immediately approached by a middle-aged, stylish-looking couple inviting me to join them at their site, so I wouldn't have to pay anything. I had already paid for a spot at the entrance, so I thanked them and told them I would definitely join them later for beer. Hell's Gate is a great campground located at the banks of Snake River and overlooking an agglomerate of rocky formations across the river. The place is very well run by Steve at a neat welcome building featuring a large model of Idaho Mountains and Lolo Pass which I was soon to ride.

Approaching Hell's Gate Campground in Lewiston, Idaho.

After pitching my tent and taking a shower, I decided to walk around a bit. I was sitting on the steps of a cabin that seemed to be unoccupied when this guy from a nearby tent approached me - the third Ron so far. Ron had that kind of look that you can write a whole book about him before he even opens his mouth. He looked to be in his early '70s with long gray hair held in a ponytail, a shaggy beard and a long braided mustache that draped over the sides of his mouth. Ron was devoid of a few teeth, and dressed as if he was either joining a Willie Nelson parade or hunting raccoons. The conversation somehow turned quickly to pot. I know I look the part and I'm often in that situation where I don't know anything about it, but I have to play cool. Ron was very opinionated, to say the least, so he soon "enlightened" me on the reason why marijuana - which he grows at his house somewhere south - became illegal. His rationale for that, and I kid you not, is that because the Blacks were the ones using pot first in the States many decades ago, the government made it illegal so they could arrest the ... and yes, he did use the "N" word of course. Seeing that my expression failed to show the disgust I felt, he kept on going along those lines. I wouldn't argue with someone who I can clearly see would never be persuaded otherwise. I don't expect to change people that fast.

Suddenly he goes, "Do you like guns?"

"I don't have one," I said, "but I don't mind them," again, unable to say what I was actually thinking.

Then he pulls a tiny little gun out of his pocket saying that despite being small that thing "shoots like a cannon." Good for you I thought, now just put that damn thing back in your pocket will you! I just smiled. He went on and on about his amazing theories. Another one being that we should shoot all the Mexicans, because all they do is "to go around our national forests, shitting all over them." And he meant it, literally. Alright then Ron!

I'm usually pretty good at not getting entangled with the wrong crowd. But this one had me. To my luck, I see the couple that I had met before walking by and I waved to them to wait for me.

I spent a lovely night discussing travels and eating veggie and hummus with E.D. and his companion. E.D. is retired and now goes around doing among other things, white water rafting. He also protests by boarding ships that are overfishing in the oceans, an offshoot of his previous work with Greenpeace. The night turned out to be much nicer than it started.

Next morning, I had to backtrack into Lewiston. Took a quick stop for an iced coffee and left town with a sense of relief.

Fixed My Buttocks in Orofino

Ride No. 8 = Lewiston to Orofino, Idaho, 53.1 miles

Orofino gets the distinction of treating my saddle sores. I don't recall having mentioned yet, but despite having been riding the same saddle for many years, somehow my sitting bones pressing the skin over it for seven or eight hours a day was more than my buttocks could handle.

It started with discomfort many days ago, going all the way to plain torture by the time I reached Orofino, Idaho. I couldn't find any sitting position anymore that would relieve the pain. I had been riding for hours under a burning pain that slowly damaged the skin, and I was then, faced with some bleeding mess. I'm getting too visual here. Let's just say that my first order of business was to find a pharmacist who could do something for me. Stop riding was not a choice of course.

I went straight to a drug store and the pharmacist, who proclaimed to be an avid hiker, took pity on me and advised me to purchase two different types of healing pads to apply on my ... well, sore area. And that's how this thing called "mole skin" became a central part of my life for the next few weeks.

Got a motel room that night that stood on a short hill above the city and behind the local restaurant/bar/breakfast joint where I had a nice

45

dinner and conversation with an older waitress who gave me my first free taste of huckleberry in the form of a cheesecake. I became addicted to all things huckleberry right there.

Orofino (Spanish for fine gold) was a great dig indeed, and the perfect way to put Lewiston behind.

Road to Orofino, Idaho.

Let Time Stop

Ride No. 9 - Orofino to Lowell, Idaho, 54.4 miles

Lowell is not a town, a village, or even a block. All I saw was a road sign with the town's name and a curious "census" data below: population 244 (scratched over), then the number 243 below. Looks like I just missed a funeral! However the road sign was located next to Wilderness Inn on beautiful Route 12 along the Lochsa River.

The sweet Wilderness Motel in Lowell, Idaho.

Sitting on a lame plastic chair in front of my room, I enjoyed one of the greatest moments of my trip. The Inn stretches parallel to the road, and every door of its few rooms overlooks the road, the Lochsa River, and a plethora of hills and mountains behind the river. It's quiet, it's bright green, beautiful, peaceful. I took a nice shower, went to the restaurant that adjoins the office and the rooms, ate a decent pasta, bought a bottle of beer and went back to my room to rest. That's when I realized that there was no reason whatsoever to go indoors. My room door had that plastic chair next to it overlooking all that beauty. So I grabbed my blanket, stretched my legs, put "Desert of Roses" on my phone, a wonderful classical piece by American composer Robert Moran, and began to take in the moment, one second at a time. As the sun began to set behind the mountains, a small deer appeared across the street to drink water from the river. And she decided to stay there for a very long time, chewing grass, drinking water, looking around, and walking one step at a time on the river banks in front of me. My classical music might have had something to do with it.

When the sun completely gave way to the light of stars, and it had been about three hours sitting contemplating the extent of all that beauty, I still had some beer left and music to listen, so I traded the lush green down here on Earth for the myriad of bright spots up there, and kept on breathing. That's all that was needed to be done in the world at that moment. If, for some reason, it had to be my last "ride" down here, I would happily join the stars right and there.

Said goodnight to my *deer friend* and slept as if peace was all that the world was made of.

The Lochsa River. Lowell, Idaho.

Climbing High for Moose Drool

Ride No. 10 = Lowell to Lochsa Lodge, Idaho, 65.7 miles

My goal for the day was to reach the famous Lolo Pass, elevation 5,223 feet on the border of Idaho and Montana. I knew it was going to be a rough climbing day, but no training could have prepared me for a 65-mile non-stop climb and 2,200 feet elevation gain.

The riding was unbelievably gorgeous. A cyclist could ride along the Lochsa River for hours looking at a never-ending display of unique rock formations, green mountains and cliffs, and the winding course of the river bringing new and awe-inspiring picturesque landscapes every few yards. At every river and road bend I marveled at the assemblage of natural features mingled with bubbly water rolling down rocks. I would have stopped to capture it all in my camera, if only I had a real clue of what to do with it.

Out of nowhere, a bicycle caught up with me as I was riding. That was Michael from Switzerland. We exchanged a few words and promised to meet up in a few miles at Lochsa Lodge along the road. He was riding fast. His bicycle was brand new and looked fit for the task, so I let him go ahead to continue his not-so-touring pace.

It was a beautiful day and relatively hot. I rode by a campground along the way and decided to enter it to search for water. After circling around twice looking for this spigot that was supposed to exist somewhere, a woman and her two young daughters of about six came running after me, offering me a cold bottle of water. Soon after, their entire party came over with more water and Cliff Bars. I must have looked in bad need of replenishment. Turns out that the two husbands in the group work for Cliff Bars so they offered me a few samples, asked me a bunch of questions about my trip, and wished me well on my way. Great families.

Arriving at the gorgeous Lochsa Lodge, which I intended as a pit stop only, I saw Michael all set up with his tent and resting at a shady spot on a bench telling me that tenting was free and showers cost five bucks. I quickly made up my mind to hunker down.

The place has an unbelievable view of the mountains on the back porch of the lodge, great food, and a local beer on tap called Moose Drool, which pretty much represents all a travelling cyclist needs at the end of each ride.

Not long after I arrived, a third cyclist, Mike, of the long, shaggy beard, rode over to our spot which was up to four strong now. His long beard was a common feature on male touring cyclists; although Mike is a finer example of that bunch, perhaps due to the fact that we were in Idaho and he was going west being on the road a lot longer. Mike pitches his tent around us and soon we have a community of the ragged and tired under the trees.

After a nice restful dinner I went into my small tent feeling like my journey was fulfilling my expectations. *Check* and *check*, next to *beautiful views* and *good times with fresh acquaintances* categories.

Oh, and great new dark beer finds, even if they are named "Moose Drool."

Lochsa River, Idaho. On the way to Lochsa Lodge.

Visiting Adventure Cycling Association

Ride No. 11 = Lolo Pass torture to Missoula, Montana, 57.3 miles

Even as the ride yesterday featured sixty plus miles of climbing, it didn't feel that bad at times given the smooth asphalt and low grades. But today, mercy took a day off around me.

To reach Lolo Pass, the highest point of the ride, I had a five-mile steep continuous climb. One of those where you wish for the summit at every bend of the road just to find out that it's not there yet as you're pressing as hard as you can on the pedals and your odometer insists on showing nothing more than five to six miles an hour.

At the top of Lolo Pass a few cyclists congregated at the beautiful welcome and information center drinking free coffee and cold water, some going east, others going west, the climb being just as steep no matter which way you came from.

Met Ginger, this sweet small lady who looked to be a bit older than me, and a bit in better shape as well ... Ginger had been travelling westward and had just gone up the Lolo Pass in Idaho coming the opposite way. We took a picture together and felt immediately connected in our efforts and challenge. Ginger said something that I only understood a few weeks later. She said:

"I'm glad to be in Idaho. I didn't care for Wyoming."

She expressed a genuine relief for having gone through a very tough state to cycle. Something I was about to fully experience.

Me and fellow coast-to-coaster Ginger, reaching the top of Lolo Pass from opposite directions.

Made over the Lolo Pass with a great amount of cool water and stimulating free coffee then took off toward the popular Lolo Springs where this lady asked me as soon as she saw me arriving:

"Are you the one whom a moose wasn't letting go by on the road down there?"

Luckily not. Apparently a moose kept swinging its horns at a cyclist on the road and cars stopped by, trying to distract the fella so the cyclist could go on... No, I'm glad I wasn't chosen for that battle.

At the unexciting Lolo Springs I caught up with Michael, the Swiss, who always seemed to be in a hurry to get to the next stop. After a few good pints of cold water we took off again, met up at the town of Lolo, and decided to take it easy and ride together to Missoula, officially making it into Montana, mid-day on July 4th.

I had high expectations for Missoula after hearing great things about the town on the road. I thought it would be a good place to spend July 4th. After we each got cheap motel rooms, Michael and I walked around downtown expecting to find cheerful and festive crowds. Finding neither.

In fact we had a tough time finding a place open to eat and fill up on celebratory libations. Fireworks were to take place far away from downtown due to the risk of fire around the industries surrounding downtown.

Disappointed, I went to bed, but not before acquiring a great tip from a passerby. It turns out that Missoula (such information that I should absolutely be aware of) is where the headquarters of Adventure Cycling Association (ACA) dwells. So I went to bed looking forward to visiting it and finding out a little more, up close and personally, about this association that all the ... (what should we call them?) "Coast-to-Coasters" you meet on the road talk about. It seemed that everyone but me was taking advantage of the rich pool of information that ACA provides to cyclists going on "adventure rides."

After breakfast, Michael and I headed to the ACA building close by. And how impressive that was. ACA has its own separate building, complete with an exhibit of old travelling bicycles along the wall. Many that looked like they had been picked up right after their owners finished the journey and were hung still displaying the dirt and grit of the road. I finally became a member of ACA. They took my picture to post on their visitor's wall and I headed back to the motel to resume my travel. Little did I know I would have some of the roughest and psychologically-trying rides over the next three days. It was time to hop on Freeway 90 for about 224 miles all the way to Bozeman, Montana.

Is Someone Under My Bed?

Ride 12 = Missoula to Drummond, Montana, 57.9 miles

Left Missoula not knowing exactly how far I was going to ride that day. Michael took off in front of me as usual and we didn't plan any particular location to meet. Michael was an interesting case. He sold his company in Switzerland, made enough money to enjoy life, and flew to California to spend some time hiking on the mountains. After a few weeks he decided that the going was too rough, bought a brand new bicycle and all the necessary gear to ride across the country instead. Michael is about my age, 55ish; around 6 foot 2 I'd say and very fit. In a sense, I think, his penchant for challenges brought the wrong character to his new adventure. He was never *there* during the rides; he was just *going* somewhere else.

Although Michael was a good company, riding with someone else changed the dynamics of my ride completely. I didn't feel as sharp. I would unconsciously rely on his eyes, attention and decision-making for unsafe features of the road, destinations, and pace. My senses, which kept me abreast of any little changes around me wherever I've been so far, would take the back seat at times. Most importantly, that undefinable "sixth sense," the one that puts you in touch with your guts; the one that senses people's and place's *vibes* before it is too late to backtrack on your

59

decisions; the one that captures the motion, color and flavor of the energy around you. That sense is shut off when you are not intrinsically focused on your personal experience.

The probable destination was Deer Lodge about 100 miles away, but having just left the mountains of Idaho, the temperature had risen substantially, Freeway 90 is devoid of much attraction for amazingly long stretches and the prospective of finding water between places wasn't very reassuring.

It didn't take me 15 miles to get my first flat tire on the road. Luckily, I was approaching a highway exit and was able to go under the shade of the underpass, unload my bicycle of all bags and gear over the back tire and test my newly-enhanced tube-changing skills, thanks to my friend Brendan who showed me that even something as simple as fixing a flat has its tricks and shortcuts.

On the subject of flat tires ... pieces of truck tires laden with small and killer sharp wires litter most of the busy roads of this country. Tire companies I'm sure are very aware of that. Sometimes you find huge pieces blocking the shoulder with lots of small debris of rubber and wire surrounding it. During my three days riding from Missoula to Bozeman I was awarded one flat per day, courtesy of tire companies. I know because I extracted those small and not so-small wires from my tire.

Changing one tire a day is bad enough. Changing them at the side of a scorching hot freeway on my second freeway ride, with no place to lean your bicycle, no trees for shade and with cars running at Montana's generous 80 mile speed limit isn't fun one single bit. One the positive side, I also honed my tube patching skills at night after each ride.

Not exactly the best place to change a tube.

At the town of Clinton, Montana, I exited the highway with the promising sign of "services" wishing to find cold water, and for the first time I rode on a so-called "frontage" road. Roads that run parallel to highways so locals don't have to hop on them to go from place to place. The problem though, is that there are no guarantees that a frontage road will have a further entrance or exit into the highway again miles down the road. And that's exactly what happened to me. After riding for about 10 miles I hit the end of the road, and still couldn't find "services." I actually tried to walk my bicycle over the fence and over the train track that separate the frontage road and the highway but it was simply impossible. I backtracked, found the general store on the other side of the town and headed back to the freeway.

After wasting all this time today, changing a tire, unloading and loading again, getting lost in Clinton, I arrived at a small town by the freeway called Drummond. One of those single-road towns with a small motel, restaurant and cafe, where you can still tie your horse at its entrance. Didn't tie my horse. Instead I walked into the office/restaurant wearing my colorful outfit and tight bicycle shorts. Not a welcomed sight around here. After settling into a room, I had a nice dinner gulping down two or more beers from their exclusive selection of lites! I can't stand light beers. I don't get the point of it. I don't drink more than one or two when I do drink a beer, so I want to get the most flavor I'm entitled to. Why not eh! Went to bed looking forward to a restful night.

About 12:30 a.m. I was awakened by what felt like someone under my bed, rocking it and waving it and the sound of the furniture cracking. I actually looked under the bed in confusion, but my first conclusion was that the dark clouds from the night before had suddenly turned into a tornado and the room was being sucked up.

After just a few seconds it stopped. I went to the window and saw no signs of wind or storm and nobody outside either. Then it became obvious to me, and it was confirmed by the only subject the breakfast patrons in the morning wanted to talk about. Drummond had been hit by an earthquake. A 5.8 with the epicenter being the town of Lincoln, Montana, 43 miles away. Apparently the strongest earthquake the town had seen. I packed up quickly and headed back to the freeway.

Just Your Regular "Testicle Festival" in Rock Creek
Ride 13 = Drummond to Butte, Montana, 77 miles

Another day on Freeway 90, although this time hitting 5,500 feet elevation. Which, of course reminds me that what goes up ... and down I went. Slowly. Knuckle-cramping style. I had to stop several times during descents to make sure that my brake pads would not get so hot as to start literally melting and falling apart which would not make for a good ride down huge hills on a loaded bicycle.

Not much to report on this Freeway ride aside from another flat tire, courtesy of truck tire companies, and a double take at a billboard by the road that welcomed visitors to the upcoming "Testicle Festival" taking place in Rock Creek. Say what?

You see, Rock Creek Lodge in Montana hosts a five-day yearly testicle festival that feeds two and half tons of bull balls to attendees. Choices include: deep-fried bull's testicles (peeled, marinated in beer, breaded four times, and deep fried to look like a fat breaded pork tenderloin, OMG!), bull-chip throwing contest, and bull-shit bingo! I'll pass this time.

Getting to Butte, as I do in every medium size town when it's not obvious where the center of town is located, I rode around for about half-hour getting all kinds of directions to where "downtown" was, until a car shop mechanic explained to me that Butte doesn't have one. It is spread in every direction, and I should go back to its entrance where the motels are. Butte was quite ordinary. Checked into a Motel 6, had dinner at a Mexican restaurant again, despite of my lack of interest in that food - although the vegetable fajitas are growing on me - went back to my room to patch up all the flat tubes that I was beginning to accumulate in my bags and to make sure I had enough healthy ones to get me to Bozeman tomorrow.

Crossing the Continental Divide

Ride 14 = Butte to Bozeman, Montana, 83.7 miles

Before leaving Butte in the morning, I found a Starbucks for a minimum guarantee of a decent cup of Americano before hopping again on Freeway 90. At Starbucks, I had a nice conversation with an absolute Richard Harris' doppelganger, that late and great Irish actor. Watch "Wrestling Ernest Hemingway" with Harris as the main actor some day. One of my all-time favorite deceivingly simple movies.

Jumped in for the third day straight onto Freeway 90 toward Bozeman. Despite the elation of crossing the Continental Divide and its over 6000 feet of altitude, and the subsequent, just as painful, four-mile steep ascent after Cardwell, this day ride has been by far the most grindingly torturous I have had. What can one say about 84 miles of freeway riding navigating every piece of broken truck tire spread through the shoulders for the entire ride.

I rode for almost eight hours, being the last day before my four-day break at Yellowstone, I wasn't in a hurry to finish, nor could I ride any faster given my accumulated fatigue of the last twelve days.

For the first time in this journey, I felt a somewhat sense of anatomical detachment between my legs and my mind. My legs were executing this automatic rotational task, ad infinitum, while my brain didn't want to be there anymore. And yet, onward they carried me. Until the last eight miles when, as a piece of atmospheric cruelty the wind changed completely hitting me head on, almost as if trying to keep me away from the city.

Bozeman

Next morning I woke up with the anticipation of enjoying Bozeman and visiting Montana Hall where Robert Pirsig taught during his stint at Montana University.

I unpacked all my stuff at the overpriced motel room which I was told at the desk of a Hilton Hotel at the entrance of Bozeman last night, to be the very last room available in the entire city that night. It certainly felt that way. I fixed the third flat in three days, and then rode into downtown, looking for Hangtail bike shop on East Main Street.

"You riding cross-country?" they asked me.

"Yes, been on the road for two weeks only," I replied.

"Where you riding from?"

"I left Missoula three days ago, riding on Freeway 90 all the way. Hate it!"

"We had a guy here last night who dropped his bike and gave up crossing the country. He asked us to ship his bike to Florida."

"Tall guy. Accent?" I asked.

"Yes, let me see."

"Oh yes, I know that bike. His name is Michael. He's from Switzerland.

"That's right. He said it was way too hot to keep on."

While they worked on my bicycle I took a walk downtown looking for a good cup of coffee - not hard at all to find it in Bozeman - and eventually found someone who could direct me to the university.

Sitting outside of a coffee shop enjoying the parade of good looking people that seem to congregate in certain chosen locations along the country - my crude generalization of course - I quickly ran into Pipen, a knowledgeable local who directed me to Montana Hall.

I walked for about thirty minutes from downtown to Montana State University just to be welcomed by the sight of Montana Hall being remodeled and all closed down. No matter. I stood in front of that beautiful building overlooking all four corners of the city, as well as the Gallatin Mountains which Pirsig said to stare at through the windows of the room he taught.

I stood there for quite some time. I tried three separate entrances, all locked. I touched the building, not having a clue as to why I should perform that act, or what the tactile feeling of my hand upon the bricks would bring to my emotional or psychological state.

What does "being" there, any *there*, offer to someone who connects that place with a very important part of his history? I could not figure that out at all. I can't really say that my material presence alongside the material presence of that building and that location meant more than his words on paper which I'm so fond of.

Nevertheless, I was elated for being so close to where much of the story behind "Zen and the Art of Motorcycle Maintenance," written by Robert Pirsig in the 1970s had taken place. I have loved that book ever since I touched it for the first time, as a 24-year-old, Brazilian, reading it in Portuguese and, in hindsight, barely half-grasping the profundity of the issues discussed in the book; not tapping, at that time, into the vast wisdom that it provides. And yet, something stuck with me, and kept a burning spark in my mind making me go back over and over along my adulthood and each time discovering hidden depths that I could not believe I had previously missed.

Obviously, Pirsig is not the greatest philosopher in history. "Professional" philosophers have a hard time even including Pirsig on the list of important philosophers of the 20th Century. But that's just a question of labels. Was he a literary writer? A travelling writer? Was he writing a book on motorcycle maintenance? Was he a *philosopher?* Or just a deep thinking human being with a broad scope of interests and a penchant for ardently studying the issues that moved him, to the point that the end result of those interests are insights that can enrich the reader in some profound ways. Perhaps I'm even downplaying the profundity of Pirsig's writing in an attempt to appease his critics, which I should not be doing. What relevance other people's impressions of Pirsig's words have to my personal experience of his writing? In reality, none. I have benefited from his insights in education, teaching and the nature of learning more than any other book I have been exposed to throughout my academic degrees in education. Aside from Alfred North Whitehead and his little book titled "On Education," I cannot recollect anything I read that has helped me as much to be a better educator. I will refrain from entering into a long discussion of the issues he touches upon in his book, and the subsequent one titled "Lila." One has to taste it for oneself.

It was with all the weight of his influence in my life that I stood where he stood. I quickly realized the oddity of what I was doing though. I could not by any degree, access the experiences that had taken place around that building by simply being there so many years later. I might as well have been on Mars, and it wouldn't have made any difference. I didn't feel any wiser for having stood there; nor did I feel like I achieved some kind of enhanced connection with Pirsig. I simply felt happy. I walked away knowing that there was no need to look for that particular corner where something significant had been described in the book. I didn't have to look for the bench with the inscription: "for senior citizens only" where he rested on his way to classes. I understood the sort of personal experience I was having - or not having - and was entirely fulfilled with its magnitude.

Pirsig just passed away a couple of months ago. I always knew that as the recluse that he was, the only way I would get any news about him would be in the occurrence of his passing, and I somehow expected that much more would be made of it. I read the NY Times obituary and a few others, and learned a little more about his life. Many people expressed the importance of Pirsig in their lives the same way, or more profoundly than I felt perhaps. But, of course, all that was beside the point. I'm living the only life I can touch, and in it, there is a thick slice that is marked by what the man and his book has brought me. That is all that matters.

Montana State University's Montana Hall, where Pirsig taught.

9500 Feet Elevation and Surrounded by the "Unwanted" Grizzly Bears

Ride 15 = Jackson Hole to Lava Mountain Lodge, Wyoming, 68 miles

After four days at Yellowstone, two spent at the Roosevelt Lodge on the north, and two at Old Faithful Hotel in the south part of the park, it was time to start pedaling again.

My wife dropped me at a bicycle shop in Jackson where some great guys helped me piece my bicycle together again, fixed two flats and advised me on my route, warning me that my upcoming Teton Pass would not only be a hard climb but it would include a grizzly bear infested area where in fact the "bad bears" are dropped from other places where they are not "welcomed." That was really something to look forward to.

The town of Jackson is the ultimate touristic town. I had to leave as fast as I could before the lure of a good time at a good restaurant overlooking the Teton Mountains and a cold beer would grab a hold of me and keep me around. Something about mid-summer in a sunny beautiful place full of good looking happy people. Makes you wanna be part of it, right?

Grand Teton is one of those incredible places that we never talk about. At least if you are not a frequent traveler you don't hear much talk about it. I have lived in the States for 30 years and never once heard any mention of this place, and yet, its beauty and magnitude is of the sort that stays in our mind's eye forever.

Grand Teton Mountains on the way to Jackson, Wyoming.

Climbing the Teton Pass was my second experience with truly hard climbing on this trip. But the expressions of support and awe from drivers and locals kept the flow of energy into my legs. Running into other touring cyclists engenders a much different reaction though.

The Dude Ranch outside of Jackson, Wyoming. Could Jeff "The Dude" Lebowski actually live here?

We understand that no matter how hard the climb, we have no choice but to keep moving forward and never complain, never forget that this is the time of our lives. Turning back is not helpful. There's very little sympathy for whiners on the road.

Luckily I didn't encounter any grizzly, although the prospect of facing one, riding up a mountain at five miles per hour with a loaded bicycle never left my mind. My goal was to reach the town of Dubois, which would add perhaps another 15 miles to the day, but having found the cozy Lava Mountain Lodge before Dubois after my grueling climb I quickly settled to spend the night there. Especially when told by one of its owners that I could stay at one of the "grizzly cabins," a grizzly-proof cabin with no bathroom or running water, but with electricity and bunker beds for thirty dollars a night. Shower and dinner at the lodge, next to the cabins, however we were all advised not to step beyond the boundaries of the lodge one single bit, and by all means, never get close to the dumpster at night. That could have grizzly consequences.

My grizzly-proof shelter.

If you're ever around the Teton Pass, stop at Lava Lodge. The vibe is great, the food and beer delicious, and the gas station next door has outside speakers playing the Grateful Dead. I know!

To Beer or Not to Beer

Ride 16 = Lava Lodge to Riverton, Wyoming, 95.5 miles,

As much as I enjoyed spending the night at Lava Lodge I wished to have cycled a few more miles the night before to get to know the town of Dubois. A little town that clearly displays the pride that its residents have living there. Dubois has several old fashion Western-looking buildings, without the run-down character and hopelessness I sensed in other places.

Stopping at a coffee place I quickly engaged in a great conversation with two locals who made me feel immediately at home. From the table next to us, a lady from one of the local churches invited me to stay for free at the church should I decide to spend the night in Dubois. It was still early in the day, and I felt that I had not yet put any significant work to deserve such a rest. So I said goodbye to my friends, promised the lady that if I changed my mind I would go knocking at the church's door, but headed to the road, knowing that it would be a long, hot, thirsty day through the desert. From Lava Lodge to my next stop it would be almost 100 miles of bare land. The ungrateful company of a headwind the entire way made me feel like I was crawling through jello at times.

I quickly passed through a little town called Crowheart, one of the places along the route to Riverton, Wyoming. Crowheart gets my vote for the coolest town name of my ride so far. It conveys to me, something wildish and independent, like the character of Mid-America.

Today's ride fulfils the ticket for a long, risky, grinding ride constantly touching the boundaries of dehydration and heat exhaustion. There was nothing I could do besides be on alert for any signs of dizziness. I rode almost 100 miles through a steady headwind that never allowed me to reach any pedaling momentum. The sun was brutal, roadside shade pretty much nonexistent and places to refill my water bottles few and far in between. After all, I was crossing a Wyoming desert. There's nothing there. And yet, this day alone I counted fourteen cyclists riding by me going west. One of them told me they were crossing the country as a group. Seeing them riding separated by many miles from one another gave me even more reassurance of my choice of solo riding. Some of them looked like they were not having any fun at all, to say the least. I was riding against the wind, but they had hills to deal with and some cyclists appeared to me as if they would not make into Dubois today. Hopefully I was wrong.

Never-ending roads along the Wyoming desert.

At some point, miraculously, I hit the town of Riverton not knowing what to expect. If you are told upon arrival that the nice part of town is "that way, because they just built a new Walmart" then you kind of get the idea of where you are at. Riverton is so far the least favorite place I have passed through. Congrats, you beat Lewiston. Riding into the parking lot of a motel - it seemed useless to look for a safe campground - I got the curious, if somewhat menacing look by three young guys sitting in front of it. So I made a quick 360 around the parking lot and left as if I had just entered it by accident.

I found another friendlier looking motel, where, after becoming human again under the magical act of a shower and change of clothes, I headed downtown looking for a place to eat and have a badly needed cold one. Riverton epitomizes - at least under first impressions - the notion of youth hopelessness, and white man desolation so often discussed in the media in regard to mid-America. That night, the town was hosting a car show around its downtown area. Several blocks were closed off to the traffic and hundreds of people walked around looking at the display of old, and odd mechanical automotive concoctions. Live music at every block or two displayed the only style publicly acceptable around there, namely, that sort of popish/cliché country music. However, what one really saw was a large contingent of sad-looking young men and women, appearing beat up and physically affected by drugs and alcohol. Their numbers were just enough to overwhelm the presence of other attendees of this town event, families with children and healthy looking youngsters. It didn't feel right to be walking around. One should not travel through unknown places if he is not hyper-vigilant to the myriad of subtle messages emanating from all different sources culminating in an ethereal energy that one feels, often as real as if one could touch it.

I stood out around there to begin with, donning my somewhat liberal, east coast hippish style. Worst of all, I had no cowboy hat on! But I was hungry, so in an act of naive hope I walked into Ralph's Lounge. Cigarette smoke overwhelmed me at once. Food was some slices of pizzas or hot dogs that the bartender informed me I could heat up in the microwave over there by the door! Beer was Bud, or Bud Light. The crowd was local and depressing looking. The pool table was surrounded by young guys watching the two players as if it was all that was left to do that night in town.

I actually ordered a pint in plain dry-mouth desperation, although I never drank a beer as fast in my life. Shouldn't have ordered a beer today. A perfect place "not to beer."

I dropped my head down and crossed the extension of the place hoping to make myself as invisible as possible.

Morning couldn't come fast enough to hit the road and I finally began heading back northeast in the direction of Buffalo and ultimately Rapid City, South Dakota ... but I'm way ahead of myself here.

Unfortunately, the good people of Wyoming do not believe in road side trees either!

Friend of the Devil

Ride 17 = Riverton to Thermopolis, Wyoming, 57.2 miles

It was another extremely hot riding day. I have been told today that "we" - as in our present civilization - have the honor of witnessing the third straight year when the month of May broke the temperature record. July feels just as record breaking. And climate change is just a theory!

Half way from Riverton to Thermopolis, which would be my stop for the day, is the town of Shoshoni, another one of those eastern Wyoming non-descriptive places featuring a few local run-down businesses, the gas station/junk food and soda place all combined in not much more than one single main street. However, in Shoshoni I was lured into a small diner and ice cream store, drooling over the chance of cooling off a bit. Upon opening the door I was face to face with an astonishingly Jerry Garcia look-alike, from the time when Jerry was in his 50s. I know it sounds so farfetched given all my previous mention of Grateful Dead so far. But trust me on this one.

I was wearing my "Steal Your Face" bicycle jersey of course. He looked at me and we immediately walked toward each other smiling and understanding the situation. I told him that he looked exactly like Jerry, which was obvious; he praised my shirt and introduced himself as "Willy" from ... San Francisco. We exchanged a few more laughs and suddenly Willy broke out singing "Trucking" as all the locals pretend not to be annoyed. Then we sang a few lines of "Friend of the Devil" together, although Willy knew every word of it - and of a lot more songs as I discovered later on at the next town. Willy and his fifth wife (if I recall correctly) travel around the country in their compact RV enjoying their lives and singing and dancing at every opportunity they can. We enjoyed an ice cream together and discussed getting together that night in Thermopolis, 30 miles away. Willy actually offered to drive me which I declined and thanked him.

The temperature was hitting high 90s again and I knew I had some climbing to do, so I loaded on cold drinks at the gas station and headed north toward Thermopolis. The ride from Shoshoni to Thermopolis was absolutely gorgeous despite the brutal heat. I spent dozens of miles riding along the Wind River Canyon, where a combination of road, river and rocky cliffs on both sides just blows you away. You simply can't believe that places like this actually exist and that you can peacefully ride your bicycle. Granted, riding west to east made it much more doable. The amount of climbing I would be faced with had I been riding west would not make this place look as pretty for sure.

Wind River Canyon. I rode for hours under variations on this beautiful landscape.

Before getting to Thermopolis I came to a beautiful lake by the road which I could not resist jumping into.

By the time I reached Thermopolis, it was 98 degrees. I headed straight to a coffee shop downtown looking for some iced drinks. Leaving my bicycle and gear outside, Scarlet was soon recognized by Willy "Jerry Garcia" walking by and we all headed next door for a couple of cold ones. By the time I had to look for a place to spend the night I was tired and groggy from the beers in my empty stomach so I went to the nearest motel around the corner, settled down, took a much needed shower and headed back to the bar/restaurant where Willy and his wife were waiting for me to enjoy the night together. The place featured live music and I was stunned when Willy took the microphone during the intermission to sing a couple of songs a Capella, which sounded really good. We stayed late, enjoyed a great dinner and drinks with live music and I reveled in the company of Willy and his lovely wife.

Willy "Jerry Garcia" of San Francisco. I won't forget meeting such an interesting character. It just makes it all so worthwhile.

The "authorider" and Willy "Jerry Garcia" after singing "Friend of the Devil" in Shoshoni, Wyoming.

Mastering Invisibility in the Midwest

Ride 18 = Thermopolis to Worland, Wyoming, 35.6 miles

I left Thermopolis committing the public sin of not visiting the Wyoming Dinosaur Center and the Hot Springs State Park. I've had enough heat in the past days to even entertain the idea of jumping into hot springs. And dinosaurs are really not my thing.

It was another short day, although the heat never lets you feel that it was easy. I had to stop in Worland given the scarcity of choices along the route I'd chosen, although I wish I knew before what was beyond Worland, had I the energy to keep going. Found a decent campground. Washed my clothes and hung them around my tent, just to have them all soaked by the rain not long after, and aside from that, I had a good time practicing my invisibility around town going out for dinner, likewise in the morning at a local breakfast joint full of farmers.

Or How the Dude Lost His Mojo

Ride 19 = Big Horn Pass, Worland to Meadowlark Lake, Wyoming, 49.9 miles

Elevation gain today, 6,003 feet. The hardest climb of my life with a 15-mile stretch of 7 to 8% grade, non-stop, not a moment's let up. And a couple of switchbacks to boot.

So far, I haven't walked my bicycle up any hill yet, although I was comfortably prepared to do just that before I started on this trip. Now it became a sort of token of pride. If I can run and walk up I should be able to ride. So I did, but stopped quite a few times to recover my legs, and or take pictures of the amazing landscape.

I met this young couple parked in their travelling van by the road who stopped me and offered food and drinks as they watched me approaching. We discussed our destinations and they told me they were travelling around the country to "find themselves," and in turn, find the right place to live and grow. What a lovely set of youngsters. We said our goodbyes and I headed up, a yard at a time feeling tired but somewhat still strong.

At some point I had to stop my bicycle over a bridge and walk down a very steep slope leading to the river to enjoy the cooling and refreshing water. I used my expanding iron bar as a walking stick, so I wouldn't slip and fall over the rocks, but once down there I ripped the benefits of cool mountain water drinking out of my LifeStraw. The thought of being able to drink river water, as I did sometimes as I kid, brings a cautious hope for the future.

If you are traveling from Worland toward the Big Horn Mountains, you will eventually run into a sign by the road, on your left, announcing the Ten Sleep Brewing Company, located at the foot of some beautiful rocky formations. Better yet, if you're lucky you'll be within the open "tap room hours." I didn't hesitate to check whether or not my schedule coincided with their open bar. It was early afternoon. The heat was brutal, and the road bare and punishing. I took their long gravel driveway and went in to check it out. I was extremely well received by the crew of Ten Sleep Brewery. They gave me a tour of the place, and let me try several of their brews. And here is the best information of all, which I wished to Zeus I knew before, especially after last night's stop in Worland. At Ten Sleep, you can pitch your tent in their backyard for ten dollars, and enjoy live music at night while quenching your desires on great brews. Route 16 around these parts of Wyoming, which doesn't seem to be in most cyclists' cross-country route, it's absolutely beautiful, and now cyclists should know about this opportunity for a great overnight experience.

Ten Sleep Brewery, Ten Sleep, Wyoming.

I left Ten Sleep Brewery, crossed the town of Ten Sleep (another one of my favorite town names), and headed toward Meadowlark Lake, unaware of the climb that awaited me.

I should probably not call it a "climb" as a matter of respect to all "real" cyclists out there who would probably just ride it up all the way. I stopped quite a bit. I stood up and pedaled pretty much at the same pace that you would be walking it up. But I can't forget that I'm carrying a 70ish pound weight under my legs. Somehow I made it to the top - or so I assumed - where the beautiful Meadowlark Lodge sits. I walked in proclaiming the lodge to be a piece of heaven on earth and the owners immediately understood why I said that. I got a table overlooking the beautiful lake and was helped by a gorgeous young waitress who supplied me with cold beer and a nice dinner.

I set up my tent by the lake behind the lodge and was warned that I could be awakened by a frequent guest to the lodge, a moose that greets visitors in the morning. But what actually woke me up overnight was a damn sneaky chipmunk doing its very best to eat through the top of my soft cooler I carry upon the front rack. I had left a half-eaten Gutsey's Boston Chocolate Bah inside, plus a bag of nuts, and I figure that damn little critter was going to do all it could to chew through the cover and steal my food. After a few attempts at throwing pine cones at that little rascal, I decided to get up and call it a night.

Went down to the lake to wash and brush my teeth with lake water (the lodge's bathroom was under construction) then with the official 49 degrees temperature right in the middle of July, I packed all my stuff and headed to the front door of the lodge waiting for breakfast.

The pictures above are from the Big Horn Mountains and roads.

What a Beautiful Country

Ride 20 = Meadowlark Lake to Buffalo, Wyoming, 46.9 miles

After leaving the lodge I actually reached the top of Big Horn Mountains, where the Powder River Pass stands at 9,666 feet high. The highest point of my trip so far. Such a climb helps you put every other climb afterwards into perspective. You've seen what torture feels like and most importantly how your body handled it and what you had to do in order to beat the mountain.

Fifteen miles before my destination that day, I ran into another beautiful lodge through the mountains, which happened to be owned by the same couple as the previous one. Tired from all the several climbs after Powder River Pass, I decided to stop for a cold drink and a bit of a rest. Sitting outside, staring at the beautiful mountains, I was approached by a couple who heard me mentioning my ride.

They were Ran and Julie, two "professional" travelers who own an RV and two cats and go around enjoying their newly retired years and the beauty of this country. Ran has a full head of white hair and a ponytail under a sort of urban cowboy hat and Julie looks like a slightly older version of an Olivia Newton John. We talked and talked and hit it off, immediately feeling connected. They love cats. I'm riding and fundraising for the rescue society and I never leave the memory of my dear cat Pietra too far from my thoughts. We talked some more, and then some, and more than two hours later I figured it was time for me to finish the two last hills I had left, before a long and steep descent into the town of Buffalo. Ran and Julie will never leave my memory of this journey as some of the sweetest people one could meet on the road.

A Beer for the Deer

Ride 21 = Buffalo to Gillette, Wyoming. 91.6miles

After a night at a campground not too far from downtown Buffalo, where I spent a large part of the time planning my next day's ride, which I did every night, I took off early in the morning without having made up my mind whether or not I would hop on Freeway 90 again - loathing that thought - or going around through Route 12, adding almost 20 miles to my ride, but avoiding the sure threat of flat tires and road depression.

Stopping at a small place for breakfast before leaving town, I heard these two older gentlemen talking about their old times together around the area and long lost friends. Figuring that they knew the region well I asked them which way I should go. It's often easy to let other people make the decisions for you. It was a no-brainer in their view, and I took the long way avoiding Freeway 90 but knowing that an extended and hot day was ahead of me.

I learned that there were only two places between Buffalo and Gillette where I could find water. After a 25-mile ride under almost 100 degrees I reached the little town of Clearmont where I filled up my bottles, had an ice cream bar and began the real ride for the day.

A few more hours of bare, dry, hot land and about 30 miles before my final destination I ran into a small old bar in the middle of nowhere called The Spotted Horse. Legend tells - I was told outside of the bar - that the actor Peter Fonda once ran over a deer around here and every once in a while he shows up to "have a beer for the deer"... given that, obviously, the story is objectively true, we are all supposed to follow his lead.

But what is also true is that you can't throw a stone in any direction around here without hitting a deer. Lone deer, mom and baby deer, pack of deer, running deer, jumping deer, frozen in place deer, daredevil crossing the road deer, dead deer, rotting deer, and even pooping deer - yes I saw that too.

So I had a *beer for the deer*, even though it sounded like a bad idea to drink alcohol on an empty stomach on a very hot day. It shot right up to my brain, but I hardly thought I would get a cycling DUI.

No matter how creepingly long, a day will come to an end. And so I arrived at the town of Gillette.

You haven't seen a bar in the middle of nowhere until you've been to the Spotted Horse.

A Sort of Cabin in the Woods

Ride 22 = Gillette to Upton, Wyoming, 52.6 miles

I took a room at a cheap motel in Gillette but found a very nice restaurant downtown to dine. In the morning I went back downtown for breakfast - the place was full, and served food, coffee and lots of cigarette smoke. It didn't seem to bother anyone.

Before leaving Gillette I found a bicycle shop in the adjacent town where the mechanic checked my bicycle, brakes and chain. Coincidentally, a gentleman who was visiting the store at that time and who seemed to know everyone was the same person I had seen the day before parking his motorcycle near me at the small general store in Clearmont on my way to Gillette and whom I had noticed looking at me. Turns out that he too had once crossed the country on his bicycle and intended to talk to me, but I was on the phone at that time.

For lack of alternative, I was going to ride on the highway that day, but at the last minute the bike shop owner mentioned the "frontage" road leading all the way to the town of Upton, Wyoming, where I planned to stay for the night. What a difference that made.

It was extremely hot. At about 10 miles into my ride I found the first tree by the road that actually provided shade over the shoulder. The very first roadside tree in more than 100 miles between yesterday and today. I'm not exaggerating one single bit. I know because I've been desperately looking for them as I pedal.

Over 100 miles without one single roadside tree.

I reached Upton under an extreme heat, and exhausted. I rode around the main street for a few blocks but couldn't find anything that resembled a motel. The only motel available had burned down the Christmas before. So I went into the small town hall where this single employee took pity on me, gave me cold water and made some phone calls to find me a place to stay. I was sent to Gose Landing, a large building that was rented for all kinds of events in town, such as dances, concerts and weddings. I sat down with David Gose, the owner, who was in the process of building a RV park with small wooden cabins around the property.

"Where you from" David asked me.

"Massachusetts" I replied.

"I'm sorry!" he quipped, so I knew I was out of my element somewhat, but in a lighthearted way.

We talked for a while, I, David and a friend of his who looked and sounded like a real cowboy and asked me if I had gone to see the high school rodeo in Gillette, which apparently was a big deal and an event that I should have never missed. He couldn't believe I didn't go.

We talked a bit more and I headed to one of his unfinished cabins in the woods. It was extremely well constructed, only still missing amenities inside. I actually pitched my tent inside given that little holes on the back wall would allow critters inside the cabin and possibility crawl over me as I slept on the floor over my camping mattress.

The door wouldn't lock. In fact, it wouldn't even close completely so I placed a piece of wood I found outside between the doorknob and the floor, and held it together with a screw I attached to the floor, MacGyver style, all that, just in case some unwelcome wildlife visitors would come overnight to check out who was inside. It also protected me from a mighty overnight storm that hit the area.

Two hours into my sleep, I actually had a visitor behind my cabin. Luckily there was a fence surrounding David's property. It sounded somewhat like a young bull having an emotional breakdown and being consoled by another not too far from my cabin. It could have been a moose doing its best angry moose call, but I was told that there's no way I would find a moose in these dry parts of Wyoming. So I settled for a buck with a broken heart ... and a Pavarotti talent.

Thanks to a real Midwestern gentleman I had a place to sleep tonight.

I fell sleep nicely and despite the awkward settings I slept past 7 a.m., took off for a nice coffee time mingling with the old guys and real cowboys downtown. At some point, the conversation went something like this:

"Did you get much rain last night?" said one guy to another.

"Nope. Point five."

"An inch," said another

"Johnny up there must have got 2."

"Oh yeah yeah… "

"Two, easily."

"Two inches for sure."

"Here comes Ted."

"Two inches."

"Ted? Yeap."

"Hey Dave. Got a lot of rain eh?"

"More than two inches I think."

"Oh yeah. More than two."

"Billy must have got slammed."

"I heard it was just an inch.

"Yeap."

"One inch."

"One inch for sure."

"Oh yeah…"

Custer a Nice Surprise

Ride 23 = Upton, Wyoming to Custer, South Dakota, 67.6

It was another extremely hot ride that felt much longer than it actually was. But it all paid off once I got to the vibrant town of Custer, South Dakota. The town was hosting its yearly festival named Gold Discovery Days with lots of downtown activities for adults and children. There were crowds of people walking around and so many options of places to stop, but in my tired, dehydrated condition I chose a place advertising a "beer patio."

Again, never a good idea to rehydrate with beer right after a ride. It shoots right into your brain and you get extremely groggy after the first pint. I had two, balanced by a nice conversation I had with two young locals who shared their thoughts about the state and the town. Truthful words that I would witness later once I rode pass western South Dakota and Mount Rushmore, which attracts millions and provides badly needed revenues to the state. One of the kids told that his state was very poor, not having enough to provide for a good education to its students. I could attest to its poverty by the condition of its roads and the look of the many towns I rode through, in and out of the Badlands all the way to the border with Iowa.

I rented a room at a decent motel downtown where the elderly owner almost had a fit, banging his fist on the counter when I proposed to bring my bicycle inside the room. I found it too comical to upset me, and he quickly remorse and disarmed by my calm response. I was tired and slightly inebriated, not in the mood for a fight, so I agreed, the price was right, and I just proposed to lock my bicycle somewhere around his property, and he promptly found a safe spot for it.

Custer was such a pleasant surprise. Walking downtown in a beautiful sunny day full of people from all over the States, stopping for pseudo-shopping (I just pretend. I can't carry anything else, although I almost bought a homemade poncho. I'm a poncho lover). Walked into a gourmet wine and coffee bar - or was it the gates of paradise? - had a nice welcome by the owner who quickly recognized my coffee snobbishness. We had a great discussion about the world of coffee while I savored a great iced coffee.

Walked a bit more around until the mob of children on the sidewalks "expressing their individuality" got on my nerves. I found a restaurant that looked just right. Went upstairs on the open deck, sat on the bar and immediately got into a two-hour conversation with a great gentleman who like me was traveling alone around the country - albeit in his camper. The young bartender frequently entered the conversation, and just as in other similar situations, I got free drinks due to my journey. By the time I walked back to my motel room, I felt as joyful and fulfilled as one gets.

"You Won't Make It"

Ride 24 = Custer to Rapid City, South Dakota, 46.7 miles

Before leaving Custer in the morning I stopped at a local old fashion breakfast joint absolutely loaded with pictures of Hello Kitty, and ... I kid you not, the Grateful Dead. How they paired the two together I can't fathom.

I climbed on my bicycle just as a major parade was taking over downtown Custer forcing me to find an alternate route. I tend to wing it. I tend to try my luck quite often when I'm driving or riding somewhere. Although I knew I was going toward the general direction, I wasn't sure of this route being the correct one. It was absolutely beautiful however, running through green mountains and monumental rock formations leading up to Mount Rushmore. One of those exquisite rock formations displayed a sign for a local rock climbing school and you could see people at all different stages of the climb.

Climbing a switchback with beautiful rock formations in the background on the way to Mt. Rushmore.

On the way to Mt. Rushmore from Custer, Wyoming.

But the main feature of this route was the never-ending series of sharp hills. By the time I reached the outskirts of Mount Rushmore I had done all the climbing I cared to do for the day.

Rock formations right behind Mt. Rushmore. Look carefully at your own risk!

Just as I reached the start of the long stretch of hills that would take me to Mount Rushmore, a motorcycle rider coming the other way looked at me and shouted "you won't make it." He rode away before I could ask him why.

Well, all I can say is that I have plenty of pictures of Scarlet and me on the top of the mountain. In fact, in a strike of creative "masterpiece" I photographed all four presidents' heads sitting on top of my bicycle seat.

Ok! Maybe it isn't a masterpiece after all...

I was truly amazed by the carvings at Mount Rushmore of course. The majestic entrance to the monument with its rows of flags along with the elegant outdoor patio epitomizes America at its best. However, the loud crowd, the personal-space-challenged oblivious tourists, and the out-of-control children allowed to be as publicly annoying as they want, quickly diminished the grandiosity of the experience.

I headed toward Rapid City, South Dakota, facing another set of brutal hills. Rapid City was going to be very significant to my trip. Around the middle of July I received a letter from the Immigration and Naturalization Service scheduling my citizenship interview for July 26 back in Lawrence, Massachusetts. I had applied a while ago and although I really wanted to see it through, I was hoping that my interview wouldn't land in the middle of my cross-country ride. But it did. I had to buy a ticket to fly back home for a couple of days, attend the interview, and fly back.

I arrived in Rapid City with the goal of finding a bicycle shop that would tune up and keep Scarlet and some of my gear for a few days while I flew home and back. Riding a few blocks downtown, I met two young guys on their bicycles and asked them about bicycle shops in town. They rode with me all the way to Cranky's Bike Shop which was about to close but the owner, a sweet kid named Zack, readily agreed to hold my bicycle for a few days and give it an once-over. Next morning at 10 a.m. after drinking coffee for two hours around the corner, I went back to Cranky's, dropped my bicycle and hung around town for a few more hours before it was time to head to the airport and fly back home.

I can't say that I wasn't disappointed about stopping my ride for a few days. I was feeling strong and very much used to being on the road every day. However, coming home for three days seeing my sister and her husband, and my friend Brendan who rode the first two days with me in

Portland, Oregon, and who was now back in Newburyport, was extremely fulfilling.

Saturday night I retraced my steps without any doubts in my mind about wanting to reach my goal, taking the airport shuttle to Boston, hopping on a plane to Rapid City, and arriving in the morning with enough time to call Zack at Cranky's Bike Shop, who had promised to open his store just so I could pick up my bicycle and get going again. But Scarlet didn't feel right after loading all my gear on it again and beginning to pedal away from Cranky's. At one point the chain got stuck between gears, and I almost crashed. So I called Zack again to meet me at his shop and he made the final adjustments on the spot, and until the end of my trip I never had a single mechanical problem.

From Rapid City I rode just a few miles into the KOA campgrounds, which is always a guarantee of a good standard of camping experience. It was too late in the day to face the huge challenge that awaited me on the next leg of my trip. Arriving at KOA I immediately struck up a conversation with a motorcyclist next to my tent who appeared very eager to talk - non-stop. Ed is an older man who loves to listen to Paul Simon songs during his rides and couldn't help manifesting his conservative ideology related to almost every issue we discussed. And yet, he wasn't preachy or offensive and had a rare ability to listen to opposite points of view. We hit it off and from afternoon all the way to bedtime we never stopped talking.

On the other side of my tent I met Annie from Bend, Oregon, who was coming back from Iowa where she participated in the popular Rag-Brai, a week-long bicycle ride around Iowa that has been going on for decades. It attracts thousands of cyclists from all over the States and abroad.

The three of us made an interesting bunch, sitting for a few hours into the night drinking beer and talking until we were all too tired to go on. Annie, as a nurse and good Oregonian, held most of her views in the opposite direction from Ed, and I, as usual wearing my conflict-avoidance hat, sat right in the middle. But the conversation was polite, interesting and punctuated with laughs, and we really enjoyed each other's company.

In the morning after Ed and I filled our bellies with pancakes, I said goodbye to my friends and headed out to the beginning of the second half of my trip, feeling like this time, I had just one destination in mind ... home!

Cycling Inside a Lit Up, Dusty Stove, Drinking Hot Water
Ride 25 = Rapid City to Interior, SD, 71.5 miles

Crossing the Badlands on a bicycle was a totally peculiar experience. The sky was faded blue, the bursts of fire from the sun reached all the way to your skin as if unimpeded by distance, and the water-starved air was a mix of fine dust and second-hand oxygen molecules.

I had no idea what to expect, but I knew it would be daunting. I ran into cyclists who had crossed it in the previous days and the overall message was one of awe, relief and pride for having done it. So I loaded on water knowing I would not find much along the way and rolled into it without any hesitation. But the Badlands on a bicycle is an unnerving experience as well. Way too easy to hide a body around here. Especially the spendable body of a lone cyclist.

The landscape is impossible to describe in earthly terms, unless you have ever lived on the bottom of the ocean, because that's exactly what the rock formations look like (and were in fact, many millions of years ago when the whole area was flooded and turned into an inland ocean). I had pretty much only one option to cross the Badlands of South Dakota, namely, Route 44 from Rapid City to the very next destination where I could find lodging for the night, in the town of Interior almost 80 miles away. Bonking half way was out of the question. I could not imagine myself, or didn't want to envision spending the night anywhere besides a proper lodging with water and food. So, I kept on rolling, slowly at first, weary of cars crossing my way which could carry suspicious passengers in search of "road features" to practice their target-shooting or beer can toss.

Crossing the Badlands of South Dakota.

At some point I actually found a little town called Scenic along Route 44 which boasts at its entrance an Old West style building covered with skulls of Bisons to "welcome" visitors.

Any wrong move around here and the next skull displayed at the entrance of town could be yours! Scenic, South Dakota.

From Scenic I spent a few more hours riding in hot flat and still very exquisite landscape all the way to Interior. Stopping was not a choice so by the time I reached Interior I was sweaty and slimy, covered in that fine dry sand that blows around the Badlands.

At Interior I found a lovely small campground, albeit pretty much devoid of trees, managed by a sweet older couple. The town of Interior sits at the southern edge of the Badlands, outside of the official national park, but the geographic features are still there all around town for anyone to see. After setting up my tent under one of the only large trees, I took a mighty shower and went to dinner at a local cowboy restaurant, which made an effort to attract tourists passing through town, but the rowdy locals cursing, being boastful and loud, ruined the experience for everybody else. I walked the mile and a half back to my camp as fast as I could, feeling "out of my element" as Walter Sobchak, a character from the movie "The Big Lebowski" would surely point out.

Camping in the Badlands.

I left the campground in Interior at 8 a.m. planning to get most of the ride done before the oppressive heat of the day would hit me again. Rode south on Route 44 for a while with a nice tailwind, a cool breeze and a sunny sky, all pretty much the opposite of what I would soon be faced with. I wasn't yet aware that I was going straight south at that point, so the tailwind made me very optimistic about the whole ride. The road was good with very little traffic. I had my music going and could hear every song due to the low frequency of cars going by, taking pictures left and right; life was good.

Then the road took a sharp turn to the left. I wasn't sure if that was temporary or it had actually put me eastward. The sharp change of direction meant that the wind was now on my side, not too bad at first, but enough to often make me swing out of a straight line.

Then I hit the town of Wamblee, a Native American small town, looking rundown and a bit depressing, to say the least. I had to find food and water, so I stopped at a food market in town which looked more like a prison with its heavy metal doors and windowless walls. I wasn't too keen on keeping my bicycle and gear outside while I grabbed some ice water, but I had no choice, expecting the heat to increase as the day went on.

I thought I had only 40 miles to go, but the cashier told me that in fact it was more like 45 or 50. Which wouldn't be so bad if it wasn't for the north wind that from Wamblee on became extremely strong. Route 44 out of Wamble has no shoulder wide enough to ride a bicycle so I had to ride over the white line, that on a two-way road gets a bit hairy.

It was more than hairy in fact. It was plain dangerous as the wind kept pushing me toward the sloped and broken down shoulder threatening to blow me over the marshes and rocks. To compensate for being constantly pushed to the right and off the road by the wind I would automatically shift the weight of my body into the left side of my bicycle which in turn made me veer into the middle of the road all the time. All that, pedaling at a very slow pace given the wind resistance, was positively nerve-racking.

Most cars made an effort to allow enough space between us as they passed me in the same direction. Some didn't. To the point that it became obvious that for some drivers, I was a persona non grata.

For about 20 miles I had the most windy ride of this trip. Altogether, there were 18 hills in those 77 miles according to the app Strava and a large part of it I had to climb while facing those wild wind gusts. As the wind died down a bit, I was completely exhausted and beginning to feel that the power had been taken away from my legs, and yet, the next sign on the road indicated that I still had 31 miles to go to hit White River, which confirmed the cashier's prediction. You take a deep breath. Your mind shifts one notch up on the challenge scale and you resign yourself to the lack of alternatives.

But surprisingly, my legs cranked on.

Finally finding trees after the Badlands.

The Hardest Ride so Far

Ride 26 = Interior to White River, South Dakota, 69.8 miles

Today it felt like the longest and most arduous ride of my trip. But then again, I have a feeling I've been saying that about every other ride. Even though it wasn't the longest in miles, the combination of a never-ending series of hills, desolate landscape and the hot weather, made it the most exhausting day by far. Alright, I said that before as well.

The highlight of this ride was a whole audience of black cows that came up to the fence along the road - about 20 of them - standing perfectly side by side staring quietly at me as I stopped to take a picture; as if they expect me to "say" something. We curiously studied each other in mutual expectation. Being outnumbered in a foreign pasture I didn't want to sound arrogant, nor say something dumb. I thought for a second. I was also afraid to disappoint them. "Should I introduce myself as *Cow Marx* and talk about universal cattle rights?" I thought.

I shouted "helloooo!" They looked even more puzzled.

"Hello Mooomooooos." Right? That's how you talk to cows.

Their expression didn't change a single bit.

"Good to see you guys," I said; I swear!

Then took some pictures, thanked them for their posing, and left, feeling like I let them down big time.

Arriving in White River I was lucky to find a single motel owned by a lovely lady with a beautiful voice. At her Thoroughbred Motel, Linda took pity on me, gave me a discount, got the AC going even before I rented the room and twice wished me to "get a good sleep" ... obviously I looked like I needed one.

The motel abutted a restaurant, another cowboy, western themed one, however with a family crowd and a very friendly bartender who made sure to find me some kind of dessert after my dinner, even though their menu had none.

Waking up next morning I read that it was supposed to rain. Severe thunderstorms perhaps. During breakfast at the same restaurant of the night before the television was on, Al Gore was being interviewed by Charlie Rose, and I heard Gore use the expression "rain bombs" as something new that it is taking place due to climate upheavals. Later looking at the sky during the ride; that was all I could think of.

My faithful audience!

Vegetarian Choices

Ride 27 = White River to Winner, South Dakota, 53.3 miles

I decided to have a short ride today. I chose the town of Winner 54 miles away mostly for lack of other options. There are "towns" in between the destinations I chose, generally, but they are often not more than a gas station and general store with, maybe, some houses around. Same features I found crossing Wyoming for the most part.

I had a pleasant ride; cloudy and mostly in the 70s, and more importantly, no wind. I feared the wind today after all I went through yesterday. The road was pretty much open to me for the entire ride. The cars and trucks going by were so few in between that their drivers often waved and showed me peace signs when we crossed paths - my white bicycle jersey with big Grateful Dead symbol stamped on it may have something to do with it. In fact I can't count the number of times drivers honk and give me a peace sign, which I interpret as "fellow deadheads" ... we're everywhere. The ones who "got it!"

Half way through my ride I noticed the sky turning darker, but it seemed to be going away from me. Or so I thought. Soon I realized that I was being chased by dark, *sarcastic* clouds. I was doing well though. The clouds never seemed to be quite fast enough to catch me. Until the last eight miles approaching the town of Winner when it became an all-out race. Luckily, I had one of the best stretches in my journey so far with a slight downhill combined with a smooth shoulder, so I cranked up the pace hoping to make it to Winner before the storm.

I was pounding down on my pedals. I heard the first thunder about five miles before town, just as I felt the first drop of rain. My rain gear was all ready to go inside one of the panniers but at this point I just wanted to be faster than the rain. And just as I'm beginning to get a little bit wet I see the sign for the Country Club Motel in Winner, which sounds so much better than it looks. But the attendant, Tanya, was absolutely delightful and after a nice discussion about the pros and cons of running an old motel, I was ready for a body odor removal through a long shower and looking for a place to eat, which turned out to be almost a 30-minute walk to the local Elks .

A note about my dinners in South Dakota so far. I haven't been able to eat well since I got back to South Dakota, five days ago after my forced few days flying back home. The "menu" at most places I eat, has been nothing more than a good euphemism for a limited choice of beef, pork, chicken and bacon combined with potatoes, and a couple of tasteless vegetables. But I'm vegetarian, which pretty much eliminates 99 percent of my choices.

I have eaten my share of small veggie sandwiches, tasteless veggie pastas, and lots of French fries for the last few days. Breakfast usually saves the day for me, given that I can always suggest the amazing innovation of "veggie omelet" along with potatoes and toast. Coffee is a dark liquid that you're supposed to accept as the real thing, although its flavor has no relation whatsoever with its namesake.

Then again, it's my entire fault. Why should I have an aversion to eating the flesh of beautiful sentient creatures who have led a miserable short life just so we could slice them in neat little pieces, package them in sterile plastic wraps, and consume them abundantly as if they never, once, wished to live?

Don't Ever Complain About the Hot Sun Around Here ... You'll Miss It

Ride 28 = Winner to Pickstown, South Dakota, 83 miles

I can't believe I'm saying this, but today I was cold. The coldest ride I've had so far. The temperature hovered around 60s the entire morning, and the dark clouds and wind made sure that it wouldn't go beyond that all day.

I rode for almost 80 miles helped by a strong tailwind. Just about time I catch some wind in my sails. Last time that happened was during my very first week through Oregon. I was due for another day like this. The road was almost entirely flat, sometimes with, or without a riding shoulder, but due to the low traffic I had no problem - mostly - keeping safe. Except for that single RV which the driver should never been behind the wheel, and passed so close to me that, had I swerved to my left just a little for any reason, I would not be here now drinking a glass of (cheap) wine in Pickstown and writing these words.

If it wasn't for a cyclist on a most unusual recumbent enclosed bicycle I would not have taken any pictures today either. The landscape in Eastern South Dakota is quite unremarkable. Not as bare as Eastern Wyoming, but the as-far-as-the-eye-can-see sort of corn and wheat farms and gentle hills on the horizon, make for a very uninteresting ride, visually speaking. So the petroleum clouds all around me made up for the lack of interest looking around while riding. In fact they kept me busy trying to guess how soon they would catch up with me and drop me a "rain bomb."

It looked pretty scary at times, but at the end I made into Pickstown, which sits at the edge of the Missouri river, where the colossal Fort Randall Dam resides. Pickstown is a very small town, but the first one since I left Rapid City where I could sense a peaceful vibe.

I did my laundry after spending the whole day sweating under my rain jacket which served as a warm rain-breaker for this nippy day, then walked to the general store in Pickstown looking for a new belt! Mine ran out of holes and my leisure shorts I wear after shower every night is literally sliding down given the more than ten pounds I have lost so far!

My motel sat next to a restaurant, which is all I want when I look for a place to spend the night. A nearby restaurant so I can replenish my calories after a long day of riding. But it doesn't always work that way of course. Often I go to bed hungry and semi-nourished over some nuts and a Cliff bar. I hate going to bed hungry without the pleasure of a dinner and a good tasty beer after putting so much work to get somewhere. Then again, with the poor quality of beer that is being served throughout most of the country, you might just as well go to bed thirsty.

About that quality of beer. It might be completely psychological, but nothing seems to go down as nicely after a long day of exertion than a cold one. Ask any adult cyclist! I love the trend of microbreweries and gourmet beers that seem to be taking over the east and west coasts. But everywhere else in between is Bud Light country. You can attest it by the number of empty beer bottles you find along the side of the road (an overwhelming number of them) and by the beer list in restaurants and grocery stores along the way. It's Bud Light nation all the way. That sort of tasteless, watered down, pointless brew that also passes for what is supposed to be the real thing. Then again, it might be the case that I just don't get it.

But I digress mightily here. In the morning, it's back to the same restaurant for breakfast. With the same waitress from the night before, however, this time she was in her pajamas ... I kid you not.

Inducted Into the Real Bikers Club

Ride 29 = Pickstown to Yankton, South Dakota, 73.7 miles

Had a pleasant ride to the town of Yankton, a relatively large city undergoing major road repairs. Along the way I met up with two bikers from New York - the ones with real engines - in the town of Tabor, a Czech town displaying signs in English and Czech. It turned out that one of the bikers' last name was *Tabor* and the two of them had just left a tavern in the main street where the locals gave them a great welcome on that account. They highly recommended the "big ass" burger they serve and I was somewhat afraid to come across less of a "tough guy" by revealing that I don't eat meat. So I told them I would have one. They gave me a hug, took smiling pictures with me and wished me luck on my trip. I felt thoroughly inducted into the two-wheel society at large! They were on their way to Sturgis as well, just like thousands who crossed my path in the past weeks. Although they looked the part, these two bikers were almost embarrassingly polite and gentle, telling me that they actually belonged to The Elks organization and planned to stay at the Elks at one of the towns I passed through "because is a charitable organization and we do a lot of good..." Those two are going to get razed in Sturgis, South Dakota, where the biggest and meanest bikers' gathering in the country takes place every year, featuring among other things I heard, three types of gangs with distinct colors that don't/shouldn't make eye contact; semi-naked girls walking around and making a buck by being slapped on the butt; and 24/7 boozing. I rest my case!

Inducted into the motorized bad-boy society.

At Yankton I took a spot at its KOA, and although I liked their camping ground, and the manager was a great guy who actually lent me a pillow when I told him I was looking for one more blow up pillow since mine went flat, and I have a hard time sleeping with only one. But the vibe around me was not right. I was given a spot next to a couple from Minnesota who wouldn't quit getting stoned with a young acquaintance who seemed to be tagging along and sleeping in their van. This guy didn't look very friendly. It didn't feel right leaving my bicycle, bags and tent unattended during shower. Something was not quite square over there, because all of sudden, this guy starts pacing around nervously, puts all his bags together plus a large and tall backpack and just walks away from the campground, at early evening. Not the best time to be looking for a ride and a place to stay with all those bags ... anyway, not my problem. Humans have a way a placing themselves in very odd situations, to say the least.

Had a good night of sleep after some peaceful writing time and a couple of beers under the moon of South Dakota.

And ... it happened again. In the morning, while having a cup of coffee with the camp's manager, my destination for the day changed completely at his suggestion. I have had a very loose conception of route in this trip. He told me to stay north toward LeMars the apparent nation's ice cream capital, to avoid Sioux City. And so I did.

KOA in Yankton, South Dakota. An attempt to dress relatively clean next morning.

Why Should I Care About Ice Cream!

Ride 30 = Yankton, South Dakota to Le Mars, Iowa, 70.7 miles

After a long ride through a very rough road under construction, and a regrettable extra turn to the north hitting a series of small hills, I entered LeMars with all its ice cream sculptures on the street corners.

About those hills. In my current riding style - my head often hanging down due to fatigue - I looked up at a road sign that "said" "Iowa scenic route - Less Hills." Yesss!! That sounds great. That sign was put there just for cyclists like me I thought. "Less Hills." But what a strange thing to say. Fine by me though. I think every state should have routes like that.

A few miles later as the number of ups and downs began to intrigue me, I saw the same sign again, however this time I read correctly, "Loess Hills" an apparent touristic route given the beauty of all its green hills!

Went to a "campground" which turned out to be the town's park again, with some facilities, but no electricity connection where I could recharge my phone, and other gadgets I carry - which include this great Bluetooth keyboard that I now type on.

The idea of camping very cheap at a place like that is very appealing. But I think it is a question of age, or being accustomed to a minimum level of comfort, especially after putting so much work to get there, I just know that I don't like the idea of tenting and sleeping overnight in a place that anyone from anywhere can just walk up to your tent in the middle of the night. Not that it can't happen at a KOA of course, but there's a little more control at the latter. Just a little.

So I looked for a motel - again!! - and found one in a different part of the town, which sits right next to a busy and popular restaurant and bar. A good looking place in fact. Perfect. Took a shower, shaved, and walked a few steps next door to the restaurant, which, to make things even better, happened to serve Guinness. Too bad that the young waiter didn't know that Guinness is a dark beer. When I inquired about his selection of dark ones, he said they had none, and went on to list them, including Guinness. Good kid though.

Never tried LeMars' world famous ice cream. Oh well. You can't do it all.

Fond of Fonda

Ride 31 = Le Mars to Fonda, Iowa, 78.4

I'm suffering from *corn overdose* - what I figure to be a legitimate and highly diagnosed condition around here. I've ridden through at least 300 miles of corn farming so far. My ride today was an overwhelming meandering around perfectly square partitions of corn plantations, followed by a brief stint of city life through the Town of Storm Lake, what appeared to be quite a nice location along a large lake with a beautiful shore, but I didn't have time to stop and enjoy it.

The small town of Fonda promised to offer me an opportunity to camp again, according to the Web. Again, the "campground" was nothing but a very small park somewhere downtown, although offering water, bathrooms and electricity. This time I had no other choice. Fonda has no formal lodging and the dark clouds that followed me through the day and that by then blanketed the entire sky above my head warned me to hunker down and pitch my tent as fast as I could. Although I would have no dinner or drinks besides the water pump in the campground, it all sounded better than riding for another fifteen miles to the next town which didn't promise to be any different.

Once I resigned to the reality of my sleeping situation for the night, I began to unpack, take all the things I needed from my panniers and pitch the tent in a nice grassy spot. As I slowly got settled I saw this older lady driving into the park, grabbing some gardening tools from her trunk and start pruning, weeding and cleaning up around the trees and gardens that surround the tent and RV spots. I ran out of water and there were no stores around to buy anything so I approached her to inquire about the quality of the water coming out of the faucets. Whether it was potable or not. She thought I shouldn't worry, and we went on for about thirty minutes talking about the town, about its struggles to keep up with the changing times, about the weather pattern around the region making it harder to farm. She told me she was 80 years old and presently volunteering at the park to fulfil her adult learning commitments to become a master gardener in town! Loved that lady.

Had a great night of sleep under the cooler weather - never rained, as correctly forecast by the future master gardener who informed me that it rarely rains around there. "The clouds just go right by over the town," she said. I went back to the road leading out of town in the morning for some sort of breakfast of bad coffee and old muffins then took off under the cool and breezy air toward the town of Ames, my destination for the day.

However, before I "leave," I have to say that, something, something!?, *connected* with me over my brief contact with the town of Fonda. I think I sort of became, fond 'of ... (ok, that's weak). I still carry a similar feeling from a road trip almost three decades ago crossing the U.S. by myself after stopping at a small town in Kansas and walking around at night looking for food. Something inside of me never left that place. Particularly one single corner in that Kansas town where I felt like my existence fully converged in time and place, in one spot, elusively but also concretely, permanently. The newness of a never-before visited location attests to the subjectivity of time. We have all experienced that. All your senses are acutely aware of that moment, enhancing memory and feeling. Perhaps that's all that is. But stronger convergences seem to take place at times. Convergences of your existence and all the features of the medium in which you're existing at that particular moment. I have memories of only a handful of such cases in my life, often in remote and banal situations. But I *existed* there, fully.

And the further I am now, physically, from that small park in Fonda, as I edit these words months after my ride, the stronger is my connection with the place. A part of me never left. I can almost transport my entire being to moments there, standing, staring at the dark clouds running fast and quiet above my head. As if that was all I needed in order to exist.

Dunkin' Donuts ... at Last

Ride 32 = Fonda to Ames, Iowa, 102.9 miles

I guess I can affirm now that corn-riding is getting on my nerves.

Riding through perfect square lots of corn for a whole day presents the advantage of low traffic, quiet roads, and enjoying my music rather than the sound of engines. The visual becomes tedious after a while, and you also run the risk of not paying attention at random stops signs sprinkled throughout the maze of roads. Exactly as it happened with a pickup driver I met on a four-way corner where corn meets corn meets corn meets corn. He had the stop sign. I didn't. I noticed he wasn't looking ahead as we approached the intersection at the same time from perpendicular points. He was staring down at his phone, while I - always the overcautious one - had my hands on my brakes. When it became obvious that he would not stop I squeezed my brakes hard at the same time that he finally lifted his head and stepped on his brakes as well. So we both stopped at the four-*corn*er looking at each other. Me, shaking my head, but trying not to look too offended, after all, the area was most likely home for him, and I wasn't going to be the one to tell him how to behave or drive around his farmland ... even though he could have killed me. But I don't think it would have bothered him much. It shouldn't be that hard to hide my body and a bicycle among millions of corn shoots.

Try this for 800 miles!

The highlight of my trip was, yes, a Dunkin Donuts shop right on my route to a motel as I arrived in Ames. I've been carrying a fifty-dollar card for 2,200 miles given to me by my lovely mother-in-law, before I could actually turn it into a nice large iced dark roast black after a hot day of bicycle riding.

I went in, made the girl behind the counter come out and take a picture of me in front of the store - I know! - And ended up getting a second free iced coffee and donut. But here is the catch. In my twenties I worked for Massachusetts coffee guru, George Howell, at one of his Coffee Connection stores around the Boston area before Starbucks held him under the gun "suggesting" that he could go out of business if he didn't sell it to them. Howell made us all study the world of coffee. He gave us seminars, books, coffee tastings, samples of the best coffee in the world and how you roast them, how you keep it fresh, how to brew it to achieve the type of coffee you want. I learned a tremendous amount from Howell and I still admire him for his love of quality. I know that I'm one of thousands who still mourn the closing of his stores a few decades ago. So, all that to say that, I find DD's coffee quite lame, weak, and in fact, hardly deserving to be called "coffee" at times. It used to be much much worse. I give them that much.

But as ice coffee goes, on a hot day when you're thirsty and sweaty, their dark roast ice is not too bad. And the price is right. So, yes, I do revel in the sight of DDs around when I'm riding. But just so...

After checking in to my motel, I went to a restaurant/sports grill bar and had a most pleasant talk with the young waitress who took a liking to my endeavor and wouldn't stop asking me questions about it.

As with most nights as well, it was time to sit down and figure out my riding route and lodging situation for the next stop. In the morning I also found for the first time in this trip, a Panera Bread store for which I also happened to carry a card. Had a nice and hearty breakfast, this time with much better coffee, and headed out of town.

Missing New England!

Earthquakes and Train Wrecks

Ride 33 = Ames to Belle Plaine, Iowa, 73.5 miles

If only they built more routes like this I would be home in just a few days. Well, that was my expectation before I began today's ride. It was probably my most direct eastward travel so far. I hopped on Route 30, a much busier route than I was told. Then again, this time I asked a young waitress at a restaurant where I ate yesterday about my choice of routes to get from Ames to Belle Plaine. I didn't consult an older and wiser local as I've been doing! She assured me that my first choice, Route 20, would present a bigger challenge of heavy traffic and that Route 30 would definitely be an easier ride. Hmmm!

Anytime someone gives me any route feedback I have to take it with a grain of salt, conscious that most certainly their impression stems from experiencing the road or highway in question from inside of a car, not on a bicycle. It has become a psychological and intellectual act of acrobatics to judge someone else's route suggestion. There are so many variables ... Feelings of riding on that freeway in Montana where the speed limit is 85 came all over me again. Some sections of this main route featured extremely narrow shoulders. Something I would soon find as a common feature in Iowa. So far, the most dangerous place to ride.

It is obviously quite common and acceptable anywhere to build backroads without paved shoulders. But here in Iowa they do it on major routes where the traffic is intense. And to make it even more deadly - I figure as a way to cut down on the cycling and motorcycling population - they pile a thick crust of loose gravel all the way to the edge of the asphalt so if you think you can get away from cars and trucks when they zipped by your left side, you're out of luck.

Today was my introduction to this type of road construction. Hopefully, only an Iowa "novelty" as I still have almost half of the country to cross.

Constant changes from paving to thick graveled shoulders in Iowa.

Once I finally exited Route 30 to access the roads leading me to Belle

Plaine my sense of relief was nothing like I have experienced before in this

trip. I'm not usually bothered by traffic. I don't think about it when I'm riding. But in Iowa you can't help hating every fast hunk of metal junk zipping by you as any one of them could be your last road neighbor! If you know what I mean.

Another trip's *first* I experienced in Iowa today was the attitude of young farmers on pick-up trucks showing their disdain for two-wheeled strangers in spandex who dare to navigate their roads. In a matter of just a couple of dozen miles I felt under attack by these not-so-funny road pranksters who yelled at me, sped up instead of slowing down when passing me, or gave me the carbon-dioxide overdose by slowing down by my side then accelerating to full throttle to cover me with diesel smoke and the annoying sound of their engines. Oh well, I figure that was the highlight of the day for some of those kids. Glad to help!

Arriving in Belle Plaine I called the phone number I got the day before when I contacted the town hall looking for a place to stay. My first time staying at an AirBnb. After a nice lunch at a local cafe I met with my host who showed me upstairs to one of the only three rooms available in town where one can spend the night. It was a most welcoming little apartment on the main street and the owner was a gentle young man who made me feel at home at his place and town, albeit warning me that the only complaint he often received from his guests was the sound of the trains running behind his building overnight. But my ears were quite accustomed to that sound by now. A large number of towns you find along your route only exist due to the railroad that has been running through them for generations.

After a quick overture to a bar a few buildings down the street for a pizza and a lame beer (only the light stuff again!) I went to bed, fell asleep promptly, and stayed that way until a loud rumbling noise woke me up. Sure it was the train, but something about the abrupt roar and the sudden silence that followed was not quite right. I'm too tired to be bothered by the "commonality" of loud roaring noises in a small town in the middle of the night. I went back to sleep and forgot about it.

By 7 a.m. I was up and walking down Belle Plaine's main street by myself. No cars in sight, moving or otherwise. Not one single person around. I stood in the middle of the street watching the shadows and the play of sunlight against its buildings. For several minutes I stared down the blocks of a mute paved road and the row of fading architecture, all to myself. Felt like a visitor who has been given a town to enjoy on his own.

Later at the breakfast place, I learned that the noise I heard and chose to ignore came from a train that had run off the tracks down the street, however with no major damage. Time to move on.

Way Out of My League - Between Beautiful Blondes
Ride 34 = Belle Plaine to Muscatine, Iowa, 90.4 miles

My goal today was to cross into Illinois no matter what it would take. To do that I had to reach Muscatine which borders Illinois, separated by the Mississippi River, my first encounter with that river. In Muscatine I would finally join the "Northern Tier Route," one of several established routes across the U.S. put together by the Adventure Cycling Association. I had bought their digital maps and downloaded it into my phone.

But before I would get to enjoy the benefit of a tried-and-true route that would take me all the way to Buffalo, N.Y., I would have to make my way haphazardly from Belle Plaine to Muscatine.

Once again, I experienced the worst of what Iowa can offer to cyclists on some of its roads, encountering that absurd design feature entirely anathema to anything on two wheels. Boy, how I would love to have a chat with the person responsible for road design in Iowa! There was one particular section that defined the whole absurdity and senselessness of those roads. I'm riding on a busy two-way road with a narrow paved shoulder - at least there was a bit of it - and just as it gets narrower the shoulder abruptly ends, cold turkey in front of me, replaced with a two-feet-wide trail of loose chunky gravel, perfectly impossible to ride over, forcing me to brave the black-top alongside trucks and pickups whose drivers were demonstrably pissed at me for being in their way in the first place. As if bicycles should not exist around there. And we are talking about a state where I heard wonderful praise for its annual week long bicycle ride called Rag-Brai, to which cyclists come from all over the country and abroad to participate. Come to think of it, I must, *must*, have somehow chosen all the wrong roads.

After a pit stop at the town of West Liberty to replenish my dried up body with water, Gatorade, and iced coffee, all at once, I headed down to the final stretch of twenty miles or so, aiming to reach Muscatine, go over the bridge that separates Iowa from Illinois, then cross back into Iowa to find a place to sleep. Which was exactly what I did.

Entering Muscatine from its north side felt and looked like so many other medium size cities I had seen so far. A bland eye-sore of chain stores and open malls edging both sides of a wide highway where the lack of any conception of architectural beauty or development planning seemed to have assaulted another community. One after another, you see cities and towns fall prey to the fallacy that an agglomerate of large commercial businesses will bring jobs, taxes and prosperity. At the end of the day you end up with a whole lot of blinking neon and concrete ugliness. The final product combines the following three things: uninspired, square concrete boxes that should be the shame of the architectural profession; wide open, lifeless asphalted parking areas; and overwhelmingly bright lit-up signs. All together a combination you just want to flee from as fast as you can. No nature; no beauty; no room for peaceful breathing and contemplation. But I don't intend to pick on Muscatine. You're not alone. We've plenty of that where I come from.

Crossing that commercial zone I hit a rundown semi-residential area leading to downtown Muscatine and shortly after I found the Norbert F. Beckey Bridge running over the Mississippi River. The bridge was heavily under construction. Little wonder, since it has collapsed twice since its inception in 1891. With only one lane left for the traffic I had to time it just right to keep up with cars going one way and not being welcomed by the ones coming the other way. Given that I could not be fast enough before the green light at the end of the bridge allowed the upcoming cars to start toward me, as soon as I finished crossing the bridge and stood by a sign "welcoming" me to Illinois, I was presented with an angry horn blast from a truck and a middle finger out the window. My first so far. Then, for the puzzlement and ire of drivers and construction workers over the bridge, I turned around and crossed back into Muscatine, to look for a place to stay. I really wanted to reach Illinois today! That's all.

By then I had done close to 90 miles of stressful, hot, shoulderless roads around Iowa and probably looked exactly the way I felt. Reaching downtown at the end of the day on a Saturday evening, not much was going on. I had seen signs for motels at the entrance of Muscatine, but I was hoping to find the purported campground at the other side of town, or at least a lodging closer to the center of town so I could walk around a bit looking for signs of human sensibility and caring. In a way I did. In the persons of two very attractive young ladies sitting at a corner table outside a restaurant. I approached them cautiously given my obvious deplorable looks and odor to inquire about the area and possible places to spend the night.

"Hmmm...." One of them sounded, looking inquisitively at me. "Let me think. I don't think there's anything around here, but if you go that way you'll find some motels."

"Is it at the entrance of the city?" I asked.

"Yes."

"I just came from there," I said, looking disappointed.

"You know what" she said. "You look like you need a drink. Why don't you join us and we'll help you find something."

"I would love that," I replied. "But I feel disgusting," I added, already taking off my helmet and leaning my bicycle against the fence before they changed their minds.

There is a reason why, even though I spent three hours talking, drinking and eating with them, that I don't remember their names right now. And the reason is "Dragon's Milk." After I joined the two good looking blondes the waitress approached me asking me if I wanted to eat or drink. I asked her about their selection of dark beers of course.

"Oh yes. We have a great dark beer on tap called 'Dragon's Milk'."

"That sounds promising," I said. "I'll have that."

And I had that, three times in fact, unaware that with its 11 percent alcohol content I would probably be out of commission to ride anywhere. Even though I also had a delicious Portobello mushroom burger with fries, all that alcohol shot up straight into my brain in my enhanced circulatory state. So, yes. I was in no condition to ride, not that I could be the judge of that, but at some point one of the girls looked at me and said,

"Well, you're not riding anywhere. We'll take you to the motel."

They helped me unpack my bicycle, take off the front wheel, dump it all on the back of their SUV and drove me over to the motel. What can I say! After a few days riding threatening shoulderless Iowa's roads and cursing the entire state for it, I was lucky to experience such a graceful send off from two young girls who trusted a completely scraggy stranger.

One more night at a crappy chain motel that offers the pretense of coziness and cleanliness. After the usual motel breakfast in the morning, I retraced my groggy route back to the bridge over the Mississippi, and for the third time in less than twelve hours, I dashed over the one open lane to piss the drivers off and finally start using the Adventure Cycling Association's Northern Tier route.

And what a difference. Once I downloaded their route into my phone, all I had to do is to follow the moving arrow on the screen. No more hours of route planning every night and bugging locals for directions.

Riding with Ganesh, the Elephant-Headed Indian God

Ride 35 = Muscatine, Iowa to Kewanee, Illinois, 71.2 miles

It took me a while to effectively get a handle on ACA's digital route directions once I crossed the river into Illinois. I actually got lost a couple of times, even though I had all the necessary information in my hands, but just didn't know how to fully access it yet.

I wasn't sure of what to expect from now on given that I was now following a tried-and-true route put together over the years by the hundreds of cyclists who crossed the country without the benefit that I now enjoy. Naively, I pictured lots of exciting landmarks, pubs, coffee shops, campgrounds, hostels, etc., along the route. Really, I was that clueless! In fact, what you get by following their route - at least wherever is possible - are quiet roads. And that should be good enough after weeks of making up as I went and finding myself battling traffic.

So let's say that from Muscatine on I commingled with farmland. I mutated into the *corn-rider*. Big league (in the parlance of our times)! If before I weaved in and out of corn country, now I became a speck of dust in a mountain of corn. Large square lots of growing corn divided by miles of flat, straight and quiet roads that went on for hundreds of miles. It's impossible to overstate the amount of land devoted to that staple in this country. Living on the coast, one often hears about the extent of U.S. farmland but you can't actually materialize a realistic picture of it in your head until you try to cross it. For a cyclist searching for safe riding there's nothing like it. As for me who can't do anything without music going on in the background it was the perfect condition.

Corn riding forever...

The weather has changed since I left the badlands in South Dakota and in spite of it being mid-summer in the Midwest, I've been donning long sleeves on most days and often a light windbreaker on top. Finding sources of water stopped being a pressing issue as well with small farming villages coming and going every few dozen miles, although one often passes by without noticing them. So slight are the changes of scenery.

My ride into Kewanee was extremely ordinary and very much eastward. Upon arriving at a main intersection I was welcomed by an overhead canvas of dark clouds that forced me to look for a place to stay as soon as possible. Not a chance to find a campground to pitch my tent which pisses me off as I'm getting sick of paying for moldy rooms. A few blocks down the road I pulled into the Kewanee Motor Lodge that was actually the right price for my budget. The yet another attendant or perhaps owner from India was very gracious as they usually are. Thanks to him I finally found out what the word written upon a metal bracelet I wear for decades meant. The word is "Ganesh," the name given to the elephant-headed Indian God, the god of wisdom and learning and the *removal of obstacles*. I wish I knew that before I set off on my trip. I could have spared some time praying for no hills!

After checking in he told me that the restaurant next door was "very good." Perfect. No need to walk around looking for food. Had a quick shower, gathered my small Bluetooth keyboard anticipating a long, relaxing dinner followed by a couple of hours of writing while enjoying a cold one. But my assumptions began to fail me as soon as I entered the restaurant and was greeted by a toothpick-chewing host who sort of directed me to a table. The waitress who came to help me happened to be on her third shift and didn't know much about her beer offerings so Mr. Toothpick Lips came to rescue her reciting in the most lackadaisical manner my three choices of light beer. Disappointment number two. Needless to say they had no vegetarian option but after consulting Toothpick Lips the waitress informed me that they could easily make me a great rice and vegetables dinner. "Our chef is amazing! I've been here for only three days, but everything I tried so far was great!" said the walking tattoo-display waitress. And there approaches Toothpick Lips holding my open beer by the mouth of the bottle! With the same fingers that jiggle the toothpick back and forth in his mouth. I look at him and the bottle, but I'm too tired to make a point of explaining to a restaurant owner that you don't wait on tables chewing a toothpick and you definitely don't hand over an open bottle of beer with your fingers around the top! There's an expression in Portuguese that may sound offensive at times but it applies so snuggly to certain instances of human behavior: "you don't call someone an idiot; it just gives them a name without changing a thing!"

To be fair, the food wasn't as bad as to beat the pasta alfredo-vomit at Linda's Restaurant at Biggs Junction by the Columbia River in Oregon. But, with its thick sweet-n-sour sauce (or whatever that brown thick slimy thing was) that must have come from a can that was probably kept in the basement waiting for the apocalypse's seven-year famine, this "awesome" dish turned out to be a close competitor to Linda's.

So, I'm happy to say that I ate the damn thing, and drank the beer on top of it - yes, I did thoroughly wipe the top. And left as fast as I could before they had a chance to offer me an "awesome" dessert.

In the morning, after a trip to the laundromat I redeemed the image of Kewanee in my mind by finding this elegant, spotless breakfast and lunch place called Damron's Cafe where I had a great breakfast before heading out of town.

Not before praying to Ganesh for a no-obstacles-day, of course!

Sign of The times

Ride 36 = Kewanee to Cornell, Illinois, 87.3 miles

If there was to be a ride when not much to say is the overarching feeling, this is it. Corn galore all over again. Nevertheless, among all that flat and prosaic ride, here comes a young girl on her bicycle from the opposite direction pulling a two-wheeler cart with a big dog inside. That was Taylor, from Maine, who had started her cross country sort of late in the season, intending to get to the West Coast at some point before the winter.

Talk about a hubris-check when you run into a 20ish year old doing this by herself, camping most of the way and dragging the weight of Dooby around. Taylor seemed so unfazed by the prospect of taking very long to accomplish it and going not more than 40 to 50 miles a day given the extra challenge she imposed on herself. We talked for a few minutes while Dooby cried inside his makeshift carrier wanting to come out. Taylor assured me that he gets lots of playtime running around. I offered some lame advice, immediately donning my "wiser" and concerned old man's hat, but she just smiled calmly thanking me for the tips and we said goodbye toward our opposite destinations.

I wanted to reach the town of Odell which would bring me to around 100 miles today, and more importantly, one ride away from Indiana the day after. The heat, lack of good food on the road, and the seemingly infinite character of these farm lots prevented me from going further than the town of Cornell. However, the real reason I stopped here for the night was that a pickup truck stopped alongside me and a smiling driver asked me if I needed a place to stay overnight, suggesting the Bayou Bluffs Campground not too far from Cornell center. I got the directions, thanked him for the tip and generosity and told him I would stop in Cornell for food and decide if I could still reach Odell. As I entered the general store for much needed water and food, I was immediately asked by this lady and her two young daughters if I was going to Bayou Bluffs, highly recommending it as the best place to stay. "Yes" I said!

Upon riding into the large office/depot/garage I was welcomed by a large "walking-smile" called Bob who brought me to the back of the building to register, offered me a free cold beer and sat down with me and his wife for a nice conversation. After showering and setting up my tent in a nice grassy spot under the trees, I was invited again for another beer and a long talk about basketball, given that Bob used to be a coach.

At Bayou Bluffs I witnessed a custom that reflects one peculiar aspect of modern culture. I noticed that a large percentage of campers seemed to have, if not permanent, but at least long term RV settlements at that camp, and pretty much every family or couple had a motorized golf cart parked in front, which they use for moving around the camp, often just to go to the next bend of the road to visit another family. At night, I saw several of those carts being driven by young teens going around the camp, orderly though, to hang out with friends. A beautiful location in the woods. A pleasant weekend. And yet, most people couldn't even walk to the next lot. Kids were not running around or riding their bicycles. Not playing soccer or hide-and-seek, but driving golf carts to hang out with friends while staring down at their phones. Meanwhile, risking sounding judgmental again, the physical condition of the majority of the people around there very much reflected their locomotive habits. Wonderful, loving people, who should not be judged based on their, often, quite unhealthy looks of course. The force of contemporary cultural norms preying upon them is so strong that they don't seem to locate the trap lying right in front of them. More like a long series of traps in the form of eating habits, television viewing, unnecessary comforts, dubiously perceived disabilities compounded by heavily advertised easy chemical solutions, all plotting to keep them in a state of

176

blissful sedentariness. It sure feels good to let a golf cart take me to the shower building. But make that a habit and soon it becomes a necessity.

In the morning, Bob and one of his regular campers had a pot of coffee waiting for me before I left, which I consumed as if there was no more caffeine left in the world. I got going early today with the certainty that I would hit another state by the end of the day.

Longest Ride of All

Ride 37 = Cornell, Illinois to Rensselaer, Indiana, 115 miles

Another nice and very much eastward ride today. I've been relying too much on that arrow on my phone's screen. Not that it doesn't work. I can't lay enough praise upon the Northern Tier Route established by ACA, but today I made no lodging plans expecting it to just be along the way. I pretty much climbed on my bicycle, opened the app and followed the roads it showed me, certain that I would be crossing into Indiana, my ninth state, and hoping that at some point I would hit a comfortable place to spend the night.

Then I cycled for hours of miles, and miles of hours through perfectly indistinct square lots of corn and soybeans hitting one little indistinct town after another without ever knowing I actually passed them. The U.S. is a wide country. The "open" land is vast, even if cultivated. The extent of infinite horizon and open sky is real, as you hear from people who drove, rode, galloped or walked across it. I often heard descriptions of vastness and never-ending solitary driving, but you can't grasp it entirely until you're part of it. You can fit the world in here.

At some point I crossed into Indiana. I know that because my phone indicated the crossing, although I didn't see one single sign notifying me of my "feat." Either way, nothing changed in my surroundings, but it felt good to enter one more state. I never thought I would be riding for so long over flat earth! You hardly ever find a hill around here, which is great for accumulating miles; not so great to prepare you for the Green Mountains range and the Appalachian Mountains range that I would be facing in a few days. Ever since I crossed the Badlands of South Dakota I have not done much climbing. Yes, the wind kind of makes up for that, often punishing you more than a hill would with its inertia-killing effect.

Indiana became my "free-range-dogs" country. For some mysterious reason the state broke the record of bike-chasing dogs running after me. Especially bad was a tiny pest that chased me on a gravel road after I had already cycled more than 100 miles, being lost and tired. Often the adventure of chasing a bicycle and bugging the crap out of a rider is accompanied by a proud look by its owner, who at times will laugh at the rider struggling to get away given a road incline, gear weight, or both.

After successfully reaching Indiana I was hoping to find lodging right across the border but it wasn't to be so. The ACA's route took me south to the town of Iroquois and a few extra miles east I entered Indiana, with no sign of town or places to stay. My next options were the towns of Rensselaer or Collegeville about 30 miles away. I settled for Rensselaer given that it seemed to be a bigger town. Well, honestly, it just sounded that way to me. I was too tired to investigate any further. So I kept going. Got lost after abandoning the Northern Tier route. Was chased by that despicably wicked dog. And finally reached the entrance of Rensselaer after 113 miles, crashing into the first motel I saw. No time or energy to search for niceties such as a campground. No reason to sugarcoat it either. The motel was awful, but I will spare the chain from naming it, and the food choices around it were limited to fast food joints with their irritating pretense of serving "good meals." But I blame all that to my being a rookie. At this point of my trip, and after several weeks on the road I should know better than leaving my lodging and feeding up to luck.

Might as well overdose on corn byproducts here in corn country. After taking a shower and inspecting the state and size of bed bugs with a magnifying glass, I walked to the ugly agglomerate section of fast-food joints and helped myself on four large glasses of "lemonade" from the self-serving machine, no doubt given my body a boost of corn syrup calories enough to carry me for the entire next decade.

Back at my motel room I had to fight off that palpable feeling that I shouldn't be there. You know you're not in your element when the *energy* just doesn't feel right; or the people around you don't exude the looks or the demeanor that slightly resembles what you're comfortable with. Then again, looks are mightily deceiving. But…. something about that energy … the one thing you have to go by when you're travelling!

All was well. In the morning I found a wonderful breakfast place after riding into downtown Rensselaer to find a pharmacy to stock up on Mole Skin pads to save my bottom from more misery. The lady behind the counter assured me that "behind the Walmart a couple of miles away you'll find a great place for breakfast!" Immediately, my sense of aesthetics (and my prejudice) kicks in, and I'm suspicious of anything resembling quality happening in and around a Walmart but I have no other option. Arriving at Royal Oak Restaurant - behind Walmart - I readily understood it to be a case of a great place that was obviously there before that big square juggernaut set its concrete box down in the neighborhood and now suffers the infamy of being known of the "restaurant behind Walmart." Enough of that word in this book now. I had a great breakfast with something that quite resembles real coffee, a friendly waitress, and a lovely send-off by an older couple outside of the restaurant as I was getting ready to pedal away.

Mexico, Peru and ... Chili?

Ride 38 = Rensselaer to Peru, Indiana, 78.7 miles

As a point of pride, today I was determined to sleep in my tent, even if I had to completely go out of my way to find a campground. Enough of depressingly moldy motels.

Only a few blocks from the breakfast place I ran into another touring cyclist stopped at an intersection, so I couldn't tell if he was going east or west. It turns out that Bob was going in my direction as well, albeit, planning to take a shorter ride today and spending the night at the home of a Warm Showers host along the way.

Spending several hours riding together was such a welcome change. Bob was about my age and was taking a loop from Niagara Falls to Idaho and back to New York. We quickly found a common pace and rode several hours before stopping for drinks and chatting, a couple of times. Not too long into our day we arrived at the home of this wonderful family that frequently hosts touring cyclists given that their house happens to be along the ACA's Northern Tier bicycle route. I was invited into their barn for a bowl of cold watermelons and an enthusiastic conversation about basketball with the kids who were big Larry Bird fans - being Indiana! - then with heavy heart I said goodbye to everyone and my road buddy and headed east expecting to ride for a few more hours toward the town of Peru, and hopefully find the Honey Bear Hollow family campground.

Thanks for the company Bob!

It's such a wishful thinking to expect to find campgrounds around farm country. I suppose not many people would plan their vacations around corn-watching. So, after riding 68 miles straight eastward over mostly quiet farm roads, I took a sharp right on Route 31 toward the town of Peru. But before hitting Peru I noticed that you had to pass the exit to "Mexico" and to keep the Spanish America theme around this region someone decided to name their town, "Chili"! Chili??? Who would name their town "asparagus," or "squash" or "parsley"? "Rosemary" perhaps. That would be sweet! So I'm still pondering if "Chili" is an attempt to pay homage to that Mexico's food staple "chili pepper" or if they actually meant to name it after the country of "Chile" to go with the theme around here, but someone bungled the spelling and it's now too late to correct it. I should have stopped in Chili to find that out!

Calling the campground ahead of my arrival, I was told that I should stop for food prior to getting there. Which brought me to a truck stop plaza a couple of miles away from the road leading to Honey Bear Hollow. After feasting on a Subway's veggie sub and a dangerous chemical combination of all kinds of liquids that fit my fancy I backtracked another two miles toward Honey Bear's way. One more dog-chasing incident behind me and I finally arrived at the beautiful campground which claims to be one of the nation's Frisbee golf ground zero. At the office, Dawn, one of the owners welcomed me as if I was a regular. She found me a beautiful spot on a green grassy field surrounded by all-embracing trees where I unpacked my tent and half of my belongings to air them out a bit, put on some classical music on my Bluetooth speaker, popped a beer and took my long sweet time pitching my tent, re-organizing my bags and pretty much just slowing down time. After a much needed shower I sat down for a couple of hours stealing the sun's light to the last drop to catch up on my writing.

I wished I could have stayed longer. Perhaps another full day to walk around, spend more time under these trees surrounded by the scent of grass rather than asphalt. You can't have it all even as we always push for it. I have taken the whole summer off to cross the country, so I won't lament over the unfulfilled desire to linger at certain places. Gotta keep on moving given that it takes longer to get to the next destination when you're powering your trip solely by the strength of your legs. There would be too many places to mourn my departure by now.

Quite early in the morning after a good night of sleep and enjoying a good cup of coffee from the office, happy with the prospect of a nice cycling weather, I headed back to that aesthetically depressing truck stop/junk food galore for another round of artificially-flavored, chemical-preservative-herbicide-and-drug-laden array of products that modern society has obediently accepted as real food ... I complied to get along with all the happy faces around me then hopped on a very busy highway leading me slowly north east. The road shoulder was littered with all sorts of small pieces of junk and I'm bracing myself for another flat at any second. Knowing that taking any road on my left would probably lead me north and back to ACA's Northern Tier route I took a gamble and crossed the highway taking a small back road in that direction. I lucked out as my GPS informed me that if I kept going this way I would eventually hit my route.

Great time camping at Honey Bear Hollow Campground.

The Town Where Nothing Happens

Ride 39 = Peru, Indiana to Paulding, Ohio, 113 miles

I made up my mind again that I wanted to cross into another state today, and that wishful thinking of finding lodging right across the border into Ohio didn't come through of course.

Just as two days ago when I crossed into Indiana and had to keep on rolling - for the more adventurous than me who are probably wondering why I didn't just pitch my tent in the wild, I'm ready to reply that "wild" around here is a farm-lot with a farmer, a dog and a rifle - but anyway, I planned this day a little better, searching the map and googling places to stay. The only option in my direction turned out to be the town of Paulding more than 110 miles away from my starting point, and, aside from overpriced hotels my only other option was the Bittersweet Inn. I called ahead, got a room for a reasonable price, settled my sore sitting bones above my seat and got my legs rolling.

I'm still riding pretty much through farmland, but the number of small villages and little towns with a grocery store that looks exactly like the one I just shopped at the previous town, gives me plenty of opportunities to refill my bottles and stomach. Often, all I need is that ice machine and a faucet and I'm golden for a few hours again. I'm beginning to find bananas again. What a joy!

I arrived in Paulding and the Bittersweet Inn was on the main road waiting for me in a bright green grassy corner. It's been a long day. Another century and some change in miles but I'm quickly in good spirits with the welcome I received at the place. I got a nice cool room upstairs, way beyond my budget by now but I've been packing up two riding days in one for a while, so I justify this type of expenses in my head by convincing myself that I would spend the same amount of money had I camped two nights, or stayed in cheap motels twice instead of one night at a more expensive place. Oh well, it doesn't make me any richer but it works to put the feeling of spendthrift out of my head.

After showering I walked downtown to find a place to eat, which comes in the form of a Mexican restaurant with a very cranky waiter. Being the single option, even though I'm not into Mexican food, I stayed, given that the place looked just fine, and the customers seemed to be enjoying their meal judging by the light atmosphere I sensed around me.

Starting a conversation with two girls at the next table, I commented on the good appearance of Paulding. The streets are clean, green and the vibe is right. The downtown park displays an oversized mural where the town's mission and its hopes for the future are written in big colored letters. What a great idea! Sort of giving purpose and direction to its residents about the expectations and dreams for their future.

"Paulding is kind of boring," said one of the girls, and they both laughed. "Like, nothing ever happens around here!"

"Well," said the other, "in fact we were like, all over the news a few weeks ago."

"Oh yeah. What happened?" I replied.

"This inmate was being transported from the hospital back to jail but he grabbed the driver by the neck, stole his guns and stuff and escaped. That was like, national news for a few days."

"Yes!" said the other girl laughing.

"Did they catch him?" I asked.

"No! Well, sort of. Hc like, hid in a hole or something at his parents' house," we all laughed agreeing that it doesn't qualify much as a hideaway, "then he shot himself."

"That was exciting," she said laughing again.

"That's too bad!" I replied. They waited for my clarification. But in my mind I knew where I was going with it and didn't feel like taking them for a rough ride through my mental musings over the media's relentless misrepresentations of society. "Well, there seem to be lots of good things happening in this town right? Looks like you have a nice place here and I'm sure there are plenty of positive interactions among people and positive things happening all the time. But that doesn't make the news. That inmate escape doesn't define your town right..." and as expected I could see that I was losing them by now. So we all sort of exchanged a leave-me-alone smile and I went back to my watered-down Mexican beer and fajitas.

In the morning, my suspicion was confirmed when I left the Bittersweet Inn and stopped downtown at the only breakfast place in town. As usual with such places, there were a few old townies and advancing grey-heads mingling about, reading the newspaper and talking in past tense. I felt extremely well received, especially considering that I don't look anything like a "regular" guy entering an early morning breakfast joint in the Midwest. I was immediately approached by a gentleman who wanted to know everything about my trip, wishing me luck and giving me advice on best routes to follow. The waitress - who could have been anyone's great-granddaughter here - kept me supplied with "coffee" till my ears were ringing and I left town with the certainty that so much happens around there.

It's just that it isn't bad enough to be on the news!

Overpriced Overnight

Ride 40 = Paulding to Fremont, Ohio, 102 miles

This shall be my shortest ride report: another flat; long, unmemorable ride; straight shot west to east, minus a detour northward when arriving in the town of Fremont because the place I was planning to stay for the night is a "drug dealing paradise" according to a resident whom I asked for directions. Had to stay at an overpriced hotel, across from a boring chain restaurant that serves good vegetarian pasta to be fair. After a tasteless hotel breakfast in the morning I traced my pedaling back through town to hop on my designated route! Looking back, the thought of riding 102 miles through completely unfamiliar places, and at the end, not having one single memory of it stand out is quite shocking. But that's the truth.

The Winds of Erie

Ride 41 = Fremont to Bay Village, Ohio, 74.4 miles

Today I entered the magnetic field of Lake Erie. The sight of a huge water tower with the inscription "Erie County" was tremendously gratifying. In particular given the prospect of soon entering one of the defining legs of my trip. Lake Erie will take me to Buffalo, N.Y. From Buffalo I will hop on the Erie Canal trail which I've heard so much for its sheer magnitude, leading me all the way to Albany, New York, near the border of Massachusetts. But I better hold my happy horses a bit.

After a few miles of backroads where I couldn't contain my excitement to get to the shores of Lake Erie, I finally reached Route 6 at the town of Huron, Ohio, and soon I found myself riding along what looked a lot like an ocean. Lake Erie of course is vast. I wasn't expecting to ride for so many days along its shores without seeing the other side. And so started a long journey of mostly flat, windy, busy, and completely unpredictable road conditions for several days. Along the lake one can clearly witness the patterns of modern urban development. One rides for miles of smooth roads edged by unending rows of beautiful houses overlooking the lake, until suddenly the road conditions begin to deteriorate, exactly as the look of the houses abutting the road start to exhibit the same decaying state.

Likewise, the other elements of poverty-ridden neighborhoods are all manifested as you ride past one fast-food joint after another, a Dollar store, signs of loitering, and the slight discomfort that accompanies cycling through such locations. Nevertheless, I keep in mind that all that, all the deteriorating state, the suspicious looks, are not, by any means, a sure indicative of the character of the humans inhabiting those places. Coming from a working-class background, in an economically-challenged country I often remember the very simple houses around my neighborhood, as well as the wonderful people who lived in them. I remind myself over and over not to ever equate low-income with low-integrity.

But the pattern is clear. I traveled for days through fancy sections of Lake Erie Road alternated by dilapidated roads and homes where, most likely, the workers that supply the services needed in fancy marinas, restaurants, and hotels along Lake Erie could afford to live.

I rode through some very nasty sections of Lake Erie Road. Shoulderless, full of potholes, squeezing myself to the curb for miles at a time not to be run over by cars, buses and pickup trucks. My first day along Lake Erie ended after more than seventy miles of headwind when I finally gave up finding a campground and lodged myself at a cheap motel at Bay

Village. I hoped to get to Cleveland today but I couldn't take the traffic and the wind any longer.

Scarlet getting a well-deserved rest by the shores of Lake Erie.

I'll Sleep in the Kitchen if I Have To

Ride 42 = Cleveland, Ohio to West Springfield,

Pennsylvania, 103.2 miles

Another "century" day, or how my friend Peter calls me now, a "centurion" - I like that!

I had not crossed a major city ever since I left Portland, Oregon, many weeks ago, but today I was forced to go through Cleveland. I didn't know what to expect to be honest. Riding downtown felt a lot like my younger days battling the streets of Boston, except that then, I didn't have almost fifty pounds of gear on my bicycle and I used to be sort of obliviously daring and detached to the dangers of the traffic around me. Or just maybe a better cyclist!

Aside from my slow going around dicey neighborhoods and busy downtown intersections, Cleveland was actually not too bad to ride through. But every rider's experience is unique to him/herself of course.

The highlight of my day was *rolling* into the Rock n' Roll Hall of Fame. I just happened to stumble right into its location, and given that I was perfectly dressed for the part with my Grateful Dead "Steal Your Face" bicycle jersey, I couldn't help but to stop by. I'll refrain from describing the place. You might want to visit it if it's your sort of thing. I didn't go much further than the entrance hall so as not to abandon my bicycle and all my stuff outside, but I got the gist of it. I walked around, took some obligatory pictures and enjoyed the vibe.

I love rock music - most of it. There are too many shades of it to be categorized as one single genre I think, but the genuine, honest stuff - if there's such a thing - it's as good and gut-ripping as a Gustav Mahler's symphony to me. However, I had no desire at all to enter the Hall of Fame any further. I immediately felt like one of those suckers who fall for any tourist trap wherever their bus or cruise ship happens to drop the anchor. What exactly is the point of visit a museum of something that - in my understanding - should be experienced by, well, *experiencing*; listening, attending a live concert, grooving to the energy of a great guitar solo, freely moving your body along the beat and the sinuous wavering of melody. It's like going to a cheesecake museum looking at cheesecake pictures and cheesecake history. Just go have a cheesecake! Oh well. Everyone is happy around me, so that's a good thing.

Dressed for the occasion. At the Rock 'n Roll Hall of Fame.

From the Hall of Fame one can follow a mix of bicycle path and alternative roads all the way out of the city, going north along Lake Erie. It was really impressive how Cleveland made a clear effort to provide runners and bikers with an extended and safe route to exercise. Somehow they found the space between chaotic highways and the shores of Lake Erie to offer its residents a bit of humane space. Not many cities have accomplished that. It's highways all the way!

I had my mind set on crossing into Pennsylvania today, so I pushed on to put Cleveland behind. Following along the lake, I went through the towns of Euclid, Painesville, Perry, North Perry, Geneva-On-The-Lake, until I hit Conneaut which I had set as a goal, it being on the border of Pennsylvania.

As I'm approaching Pennsylvania the weather begins to change. Just a few miles before the border I was still riding in short sleeves displaying my now famous jersey when a dude on his car slows down by me, asked me the usual questions about my trip, destination, told me about his love of the Grateful Dead and then asked me to keep on riding in front of his car so he could take a picture of me on my bicycle proudly wearing our common symbol of devotion. We parted ways waving to each other with big smiles, certain of our brotherhood in this planet!

Had he run into me just five miles ahead, he would have never seen my jersey, which was then hidden under two layers of rain gear. (A clarification: lest you should all think I'm wearing the same jersey every day, I do carry two bike jerseys, a white and a blue one, and they both, yes! exhibit a big "Steal Your Face" design.)

The rain came down heavily. I stopped to put on my waterproof shoe-covers and pants because I was determined to keep on going. Had all sorts of flashing lights on to alert texting-happy teenagers driving around. I rode past a small bustling touristic downtown full of surf shops, ice cream parlors, cafes and t-shirt stores, but I couldn't stop to enjoy the vibe 'cuz the rain was pouring down on my head and I felt too miserable to stop. At some point, as the rain let off a bit, on a long stretch of a highway past Conneaut, I finally entered Pennsylvania. I was closing in on another 100 mile day and didn't feel like going much longer, but my goal was another twenty or so miles to reach the town of North Springfield for the night, following Route 5 north, which I had been on for hours. And then the rain really turned into a waterfall. I rode up on Route 5 for a couple of extra miles but soon realized that I could not go any further with that kind of storm, so I stopped under the roof of an old building and searched on my phone for any motels around me. For some amazing luck and the help of Zeus of course, there was one about five miles south of where I was. Looking at the sky it didn't seem like the rain was going anywhere so I decided to enjoy nature's free shower and head toward the motel. The rain was still quite heavy when I entered the motel's office. I was completely soaked, looking like the guest from hell. I had no other option. I was cold and tired.

"I will sleep in the kitchen if I have to!" I told the lady behind the counter hoping she would have a room for me. She sort of sympathized with my plight! I guess she wasn't too keen about the prospect of a muddy wacko on his muddy bicycle taking a clean room in her motel. Then I put down my phone over her desk with the picture of my late furry baby Pietra showing as a screensaver. Her attitude changed. She loved me on the spot. We exchanged cat stories for a while then she gave me a nice room, helped me do all my soaked dirty laundry and provided me with a phone number to order pizza for dinner.

In one single day I experienced the joy of my unofficial membership into the cat-loving and Dead-loving brotherhoods of men and women.

My Kind of Town

Ride 43 = West Springfield, Pennsylvania to Westfield, New York, 61.6 miles

My third state in three days. Not much to brag given that this stretch of Pennsylvania along Lake Erie is really no more than a day's ride on a bicycle. But I was happy to be entering New York State today keeping in mind that it borders Massachusetts. It hasn't felt as doable to finish this coast-to-coast as it did today.

Riding the Penn section of Lake Erie was really pleasant. It offers you the best road conditions I have seen bordering the lake, and the prominent feature of this route was the large number of wineries along Route 5. Of course I had to stop to taste some of the local wine and give them my ludicrous input.

Following the shores of the lake on this beautiful day and after an elated picture below the "Welcome to New York" road sign, I stumbled into the town of Westfield. Or at least the section of the town I could see, which edges the lake. At a main quiet intersection I stopped at a convenience store for drinks and discovered that a KOA campground was just two miles further north. And a short downhill behind the store, toward the shore of the lake, I found a couple of restaurants and a marina.

It all sounded perfect. I rode toward the campground and got a beautiful grassy spot. After a shower I took a walk back in the direction of the marina, found a nice small restaurant with outdoor tables, right across another eating place from which I could hear live music. After dinner and a couple of great dark beers, I went to check out the place across the street and found a lovely outdoor patio with several tables overlooking the sandy beach of Lake Erie where kids were playing volleyball, and on the opposite end of the patio a musician was performing popular tunes on his guitar, accompanied by an electronic drum machine and this thing that harmonized his own voice so he could sound like a small band anytime he pushed that button. Better yet, he played several Crosby, Stills and Nash songs.

I sat down, ordered another beer and enjoyed the music - along with a humongous dessert that caused the whole bar to follow the sight of it being brought to me. Oh well, I earned it! And proudly ate it all.

To my delight, I was soon approached by the couple that owns the KOA who was also enjoying the place and offered to drive me back to their campground whenever I wanted to leave.

The food was great, the vibe perfect, the view glorious and the people around me gentle. All I can say is, if you're anywhere around Westfield, New York, stop by. You won't regret it.

Enjoying the vibe in Westfield, N.Y., on the shore of Lake Erie.

Thanks for the Dinner

Ride 44 = Westfield to Tonawanda, New York, 80.6 miles

It pays to look miserable, cold, tired and wet sometimes. You might score a free dinner paid for, anonymously. But I'm ahead of myself. Had to go through Buffalo, N.Y., before thinking of dinner, and that wasn't easy or fun at all.

I left the KOA in Westfield again with that feeling of leaving a very good thing behind me. Someday I've got to stop by again. All I had to do today was follow Route 5 pretty much all the way to Buffalo, looking to my left at the beautiful Lake Erie anytime I wanted. But things got much rougher as I approached Buffalo, by far one of the toughest cities to ride I have encountered. Unless there's another way to stick to its shore all the way to Canalside, the touristic spot in Buffalo where I was hoping to reach the final trail leading me to the Erie Canal.

As far as I could tell from researching and gathering information from locals before I hit the city, once you get close to Buffalo along Lake Erie, you can't go any further north due to a bridge that one can't cycle over. So I followed a Google cycling route that took me through some rough neighborhoods and messy roads for many miles. The traffic was intense all the way, and the chances to get *doored* at any moment were always present (if you ever rode a bicycle right passed a parked car and feared someone would open the door just as you are about to pass it, you know what I'm talking about). But I made it to the Canalside thinking that all my problems were solved once I got there. The truth is, the start of the bicycle path is sort of hidden away from where the action is. You have to go back under overpasses and heavy traffic, get on your knees to pray to Ganesh, recite a sacred chant, and look around some more ... who knows. I got lost again because not even Google maps could direct me to the trail. I consulted a local cyclist riding around and although he seemed to be an avid biker, he couldn't tell me how to get there either. It turns out that I wasn't too far from the trail but that old genius human invention called "road sign" hadn't quite caught on up here, I guess. When I finally found myself riding on the trail I soon realized it ended abruptly just a couple of miles up the road.

I stopped a couple riding in front of me, and they volunteered to lead me out of the city through the "trail" which turned out to be a combination of broken sidewalk, busy roads, riding against the traffic, and trial and error to find patches of trail that ran along the river again. At some point this gentle couple found their destination in the form of a restaurant along the shore, but by then I had less than ten miles left to the town of Tonawanda where the Erie Canal and the canal trail along its shores crossing almost the entire state of New York was supposed to begin. I rode the last few miles, still asking passerbys here and there for directions to the Erie Canal thinking that it was as popular as Niagara Falls around these parts. But in fact, most people don't know much about its whereabouts. It's there. It's huge, but aside from a whole lot of expensive real estate opportunities along its shore, the canal is pretty much obsolete these days.

As I'm approaching Tonawanda, the black clouds that often build up over Niagara caught up with me, even though I tried to overrun them. Not far from a popular pub that was my point of reference to find the Erie Canalway the rain dropped down on me as if the rain gods meant to rid me off my foul body odor.

Oh well, I guess I'll have to lean my bicycle against their fence and go in for a pint or two and some fuel. All paid for, it turned out, by an anonymous guest who sympathized with my state and heard me talking to the bartender about my trip. Data point: lots of bartenders are cyclists! This is not a scientific conclusion yet, just inductive logic, a repeated pattern that has worked in my favor quite often granting me free pints. Tip: when traveling by bicycle, talk to bartenders.

Another night spent at a god-forsaken motel not too far from the pub. In the morning, after a visit to a nearby Dunkin' Donuts where two Indian-looking kids amused themselves behind the counter trying to sound wisecracking beyond their years at the expense of half-asleep customers like me, I finally, finally ... roll onto the trail of the Erie Canal.

The Canalway along the Erie Canal where I would spend the next 300 miles.

Flat in New York

Ride 45 = Tonawanda to Rochester, New York, 89.2 miles

My introduction to the Canalway along the Erie Canal came in the experience of getting lost not long into the ride. New York is really trying to save money on road signs.

The start of the Canalway in Tonawanda, N.Y.

With one of the greatest bicycle/running trails in the country, one would expect to never getting lost. But the reality is quite different. I found myself hitting several intersections along its course where I could find no indication whatsoever as to where I should proceed to find the trail again. This pattern kept happening throughout the entire Canalway. At the same time that one could ride for hours on end without any concern with where to turn next, the occurrence of sudden blind endings along the trail added an immense amount of time to each day's ride making me go right, backtrack, go left, backtrack, try right again a bit farther this time, and so on, until I accidentally found my way.

On the other hand ... what a great place to ride your bicycle when things are working! As I said, I would ride for hours sometimes without running into anybody, or maybe a couple of runners or cyclists. Every once in a while you go by a small town along the canal. Actually, make it a bunch of small towns throughout the more than 300 miles I rode through this trail (trail/road connections that is). The little towns were my favorite in fact. One often finds a small cafe along the shore of the canal, or some stores a couple of blocks off the trail and these places often look extremely quaint.

In fact, I don't recall any town edging the Erie Canal that looked necessarily bad.

At times, the Canalway becomes nothing but a narrow double trail.

Which comes to my next subject: the city of Rochester that turned out to be my destination for the day? Note to my future-biking-self: never make your final destination for the day on a cycling touring, a big city. Plan on stopping right before, long before, right after, or long after. See, you have at least four choices not counting the two perpendicular options.

But I'm ahead of myself again.

In one of these funky road connections that take you from one section of the Canalway to another, I had to cross a busy section of a medium size town; I don't recall its name. I had to cross the overpass under a major highway and its shoulders were littered with pieces of metal from tires, car crashes and garbage. I could almost hear my tires begging me to change route but I couldn't do it. Sure enough, a couple of blocks away the wheel is hitting the ground without the benefit of a pumped up tire to shield it. It's one of the worst feelings for a cyclist. The smooth rolling of rubber against the road is substituted by a dry, sharp sequence of thuds and bumps as metal hits small rocks and cracks on the road.

No biggy right! By now I'm an expert on changing tubes. Except that now I have a brand new Schwalbe Marathon Plus tire designed for rough riding. It's a sturdy, thick tire, supposed to be non-puncturing and on top of its strength my tire was replaced just a few weeks ago at a bike store. So, the problem is that I don't have the professional tools and much less the slick skills of bike mechanics to easily refit the tire back into the wheel once the tube is replaced. An action that is usually done by the sheer strength of fingers and the rolling of your wrist to fit the tire into place. It looks easy when I see those guys doing it, but for the life of me, it's so freaking hard when you haven't done it often. You're not supposed to stick a tire lever between the tire and the wheel and yank the tire into its groove. If you have ever done that you know that most likely you will be squeezing the lever over the brand new tube, then you press it very hard against the metal of the wheel, and you just gifted yourself with one more flat tube. It's a muscle power job, combined with expertise. Long story: I'm sitting in front of the door of a church under ninety degree weather with all my gear spread around the grass, so I could get at this particular flat in my back tire, and I'm sweating like a ... (insert your cliché here). I'm drenched. I'm trying to get this hard tire back into place for what it felt like almost 30 minutes and I'm losing my cool. I haven't cursed in front of the church yet. I think. But at some point, I did commit the sin of trying to use the tire levers to fit-in the tire, although I'm so afraid of destroying another tube that I gave up halfway through.

I'm pissed. I try to keep my cool and tell myself that it's not a life or death situation, but then I remember that staying in front of that church on a funky neighborhood on a busy road was not an option either. So, it is at least sort of life-inhibiting situation. I squeeze the damn thing. I twist and push, and twist it up some more. I lose strength and I'm getting blisters from rolling my skin over the tire. I catch my breath. I look around to see if there are any signs of possible miracles ... then I go for it with life or death desperation. The bastard gives in and goes into the groove of the wheel ... and I am game again. Now it's just pumping the tire to make sure that I didn't pierce the tube with my attempts at it with the levers. Ok. All good. I'm good to roll. Miracles do happen; I just didn't think they would affect a non-believer!

After having left the safety and comfort of the Canalway I stopped at a joint in downtown Rochester for food and libations and to search for a place to spend the night. After a few phone calls, I settle for what it seemed like a good and affordable motel a few miles away and very much in the direction I had to take in the morning anyway. Towpath Motel was just fine. Just the usual drug-dealer-sleeping-next-door looking inquisitively at you wondering if you're going to buy their product, type of motel. Aside from that, I had a good night of sleep, left early in the morning, stopped at a nearby Starbucks for a half-decent cup of coffee and was approached by this lady cyclist who sat down to talk for about one hour wanting to know everything about my trip. I like to think that I have inspired a person or two along the way to give the cross-country ride a shot. She left very excited about it and told me that she would seriously consider riding across the country at some point.

Other times the Canalway, it's nothing but a single trail.

Tried My Best to Camp Today

Ride 46 = Rochester to Weedsport, New York, 76 miles.

My misguided "let-me-test-my-luck-with-lodging-for-the-night" -self, kicks in again. There were some scant choices of campgrounds along my route today.

At several sections of the ride the trail was non-existent and it was often followed by hidden starts and ends. To be fair, one finds many little purple signs displaying the word "Canalway" throughout the route across the state but they are often placed in locations where one could go pretty much in any direction. Someone has got to take a hard look into this road-sign business in New York upstate for goodness sake. But I don't want to project the impression that the Canalway, when you're actually riding it, isn't absolutely fantastic. One rides through smoothly packed dirt surrounded by nothing but woods and the river for long, long stretches. If, like me, you're into listening to your favorite songs (and if your selection happens to be as groovy as mine!) you're simply tripping through the whole trip.

Finally, through some ins and outs of roads and trail, I arrive at the town of Weedsport and head to River Forest Park Campground. How peculiar that the word "campground" is slapped onto many RV sites raising the expectations for the prospective guest that you'll actually find a "campground" instead of what is in actuality more like a mobile home away from home - no, make that a permanent home - to this sort of alternative community that chooses to live in that environment. Nothing too bad. Just different. Not necessarily a tent heaven though.

I paid forty dollars for a spot and was directed to my assigned location. I rode around the grounds for a long while until I finally figured out where the place I was supposed to pitch my tent was located. Their sense of numerical sequencing is unique to themselves. Amazingly, they gave me a small location between two permanent RVs, devoid of any grass, and in fact covered with pebbles. "Is this for real" I'm thinking to myself. "Don't they do this sort of thing for living?" I went back to the office and explained to them that travelling on a bicycle with a very small tent; I don't carry a large or thick mattress and would not be able to sleep on that ground. Duh!! So they gave me another spot, this time, as they showed me the location from the office, it looked like a grassy spot, although, with no shade whatsoever, but they promised I would find electricity given that, as I explained, I needed to recharge my phone in order to find my route. "Sure there is electricity" they said.

So, I headed to my spot, unpacked some of my bags, and tent, grabbed my extension to hook it up at the electric outlet, just to find out that it only featured those large three-pronged slits designed for RVs. I gave up. Packed all my stuff again, went back to the office, asked my money back, and rode back downtown to, again, pay for another night at a motel. A nice and clean one with a decent breakfast at least.

In the morning I stopped at a local Dunkin Donuts (they might have to pay me for all this free product placement), and not too long after found the entrance to the Canalway again.

Chased by Tornados

Ride 47 = Weedsport to Verona, New York, 65 miles

Knowing that I had to cross Syracuse at some point, I made sure that it would not be my destination for the day. Having heard from area residents that Syracuse would be pretty much like Rochester in terms of size and traffic, and let's just say, a bit of the same messiness, I just wanted to get through as fast as possible. Which was not realistic given that, just like Rochester, the canal trail stops before one gets to Syracuse and picks up again somewhere, god only knows, after you cross the entire city. But I gotta give it to Syracuse for its downtown bicycle lanes. Really well marked, strongly painted on the ground so as not to leave any doubts that cars should not be riding over it.

Congratulations Syracuse!

I had to find a bike shop to replace my cleats again. Wish I had purchased metal ones before the start of my trip, which would require a different type of pedals as well, so it's too late at this point to do it. By the time I arrived at the bike shop my cleats simply would not stay connected to the pedals anymore and my foot kept jumping off the pedal, making for very dangerous pedaling.

Finding the bike store I realized that it was located on the second floor of a building, with only a steep and narrow staircase leading up to it. I tried a couple of steps up, but being already exhausted I just couldn't get my bicycle with all my gear up the stairs. I let go an involuntary and loud growl out of frustration down there, and immediately a couple of guys showed up at the top of the stairs to check out what the barking was about. One of them grabbed my bicycle with all the gear and, probably having done that before, carried it all upstairs. At the end, I had to thank them profusely for the help with my bicycle and putting me on the right path to leave the city and find the trail again.

The weather seemed just fine, given that I've been staring toward east the entire time, so I had no idea of what was cooking behind me until I stopped at a small museum along the canal to ask for some water and the director asked me:

"You do know about the tornado warning coming up this way don't you?"

"You're kidding right" I said.

"Let me show you here on my phone," she replied.

We looked it up and it came down to this. I needed at least two hours to reach my final destination; according to the weather report, the storm with possible tornados was about one hour away from where I was at that moment. Doing the quick math, and the general speed of a storm (about the regular speed of a car ride I was told), I figured I could ride for about one hour and thirty minutes before it became critical... all things staying the same.

"You better get going," she said. Ok, too bad I had to leave. She was the very epitome of a museum director. Elegant, with an intelligent face, a mellow voice, and a positively classy demeanor. Suddenly I felt very interested in their paintings! But I had to go.

Hopping back on the trail, I could not conceive the possibility of a big storm reaching me. The day was simply perfect, but there was something brewing behind me for sure. At some point, the trail ended, and my fast and productive, straight east ride became touch and go again through back roads of small towns ... and the clouds found me big time by then.

I kept analyzing their progression and the direction of the wind. I thought for sure that the storm was going north east while I was going straight east. At some point it became obvious I had to make some decisions. I reached a major intersection at the town of Verona where a large gas station, general store, restaurant and game room were located. I locked my bicycle outside and went inside to assess the situation. I found a television that happened to be showing the weather channel and the upcoming storm. I got myself something to eat and drink and sat down in front of the TV to understand what was going on.

There were tornado warnings all around the area. And they kept showing this storm that was about to hit my present location. Well, perfect I thought. I'm inside, safe and dry and the storm should eventually go by allowing me to continue my ride. I kept staring at the TV for about 30 minutes as the rain picked up outside. So far, my plan was working perfectly. Hunker down and all shall be well.

That's when the weatherman casually reported on the second heavy storm coming right after this one. Damn... I'm sitting there the entire time thinking that I would soon be ok, just to find out that I might not be able to leave anytime soon, and possibly not until it was dark out because of the this second storm that took them forever to even mention.

I searched my phone quickly and found a hotel about five miles away. I called them and the gentleman at the desk asked me how far I was from there. I told him I was biking. He said. So get on the road right now and you might still make it. "Good luck" he added. Well, it came down to luck alright.

I hit the road toward the hotel, and just at about two miles the rain picked up with a vengeance. Another half-mile and it became impossible to ride. The wind and the rain teamed up against me now. Cars were all stopping. I could barely stay up. A looked ahead of me and saw what it looked like an industrial park with several buildings. To my unbelievable luck, there was an enclosed bus stop at the corner about 20 yards away from me. The odds of finding such a structure at that particular moment were so not good. And yet, there it was. I got off my bicycle and crossed the street, pushing it against the punishing wind and rain. I quickly went into the bus stop structure and closed the door. But the wind blew it open with a bang. I was completely soaked by them. I propped my bicycle against the back wall and leaned my body with all my strength against the door, but I could barely keep it closed. It felt like nothing but a tornado. Suddenly a couple of girls come running in from god knows where, so I opened the door for them and proceeded to lean against it to hold up the rain and wind. I was just waiting for the whole structure to take flight at any second.

That went on for about ten minutes. Then all was calm again ... and flooded. I grabbed my bicycle, and under a bit of light rain, resumed my ride to the hotel. Not surprisingly, there were downed branches and trees all over the area. Road signs had been felled by the wind everywhere. All roads were littered with debris all the way to the hotel.

Arriving at the hotel, the kind looking gentleman behind the counter realized at once who I was and what I had been through. He told me that a microburst hit the area (meaning, hit me!). By then, it was pretty obvious to me. Call it a microburst or a freaking tornado (or Gore's rain bomb!!). It didn't matter at that point. All I knew was that I had made it to safety out of sheer luck given all the trees and branches that could have hit my head, had I not found that bus stop.

In the morning, heading back toward my original route from the day before, I could see the extent of the damage around the area. Aside from all the trees and branches and roofs that were affected, I rode by a house where their unattached garage was completely flipped upside-down. Talk about luck!

Did Someone Piss on the AC Unit?

Ride 48 = Verona to Amsterdam, New York, 95.6 miles

Woke up in that nice (for my cyclist standards) "micro motel" in Verona with the weather just perfect. I little bit cool; just enough for a light windbreaker vest that I fortunately decided to bring with me at the last minute.

I had a gut-stuffing breakfast at the motel in the morning, which usually never offer anything special, but you can always eat as much as you want of what they have... and since I knew that I would easily burn it all during, at minimum, half of my ride, I eat twice of everything. The highlight of their breakfast was actually a large bowl of fruit, which I never found anywhere between east and west coasts. Fruits are pretty much non-existent in the menus of Mid-America. I was told that it's very difficult to keep them fresh, but I suspect that, just as with most things in life, "out of sight, out of mind."

On that subject: I have witnessed first-hand, a population of extremely unhealthy looking people between the two coasts. I cannot exaggerate the issue. However, I really cannot subscribe to the easy interpretation that people are just lazy or disinterested. In my view, and judging by simple observations, it's much more complex than that. Current *cultural norms* are all heavily stacked against individuals being physically active and eating healthy. It's obvious that the vast majority of the population is simply living the life that is readily available to them with all the small elements that combine to conspire against the health of their bodies (and often their minds). But it's the strength and multitude of these detrimental elements that bring a false sense of normality and unexamined subjugation into people's lives, and not, as it's often judged, a simplistic case of lack of will. My opinion!

After a quiet and gentle ride through farmland displaying the effects of last night's storm, I had to cross through Utica facing again the challenge of finding my way through and out of a large city and back onto the Erie Canalway without the benefit of directions. There's a fundamental flaw affecting the Canalway. As much as I am so impressed, and immensely grateful to New York for providing a way for cyclists to cross almost the entire state through quiet and quaint trails along the river, I can't help to point out that the canal is interrupted exactly when we need it the most. In short, when cyclists are trying to get past the big cities along the way like Rochester, Syracuse, Utica, Schenectady and into Albany, it's exactly when we are tossed right into the thick of the traffic. I can only imagine the difficulty of cutting a trail through the immensity of established and expensive properties along the canal in those big cities, but, somehow, for the sake of the other half of human movement through the planet (walkers, runners and cyclists), safe routes for us should be in the minds of every person working within a department of transportation in this country. They should give full consideration to the entire scope of their job, namely motorized and non-motorized travelling, and not, just one-half of it, as it seems to be the case in most parts of the country and the world.

After very slow movement through the traffic of Utica I got going again and spent the next sixty miles travelling on the canal, arriving late afternoon in Amsterdam, a town I didn't see much, but which I heard from some of its residents, as I did in many other places in America, that it "used to be a great town, but now…"

I stopped at a small bar near the canal where three gentlemen sitting at an outdoor table, stylishly and peacefully, shared a bottle of wine. I asked them for information about where to go.

Downtown was one way, motels were the opposite way, that also happened quite often, so I chose motels first, taking me to the highest section of town. It almost defeated me. I will explain. So far, I haven't dismounted and walked up any hill or mountain yet. I biked up every single

227

one of them. But as I'm going to the available motel I hit this short, sharp and steep hill, one of those that your car would never make it in a snowy day ... but I made it up, and then, there was another one, a bit longer right after. I knew I would bonk and get beaten, so I took a longer way around it with an easier climb. Yes, I cheated a bit, but at least it didn't ruin my pride!

My motel, just as many others I stopped by, seemed to be a home away from home for construction workers at a price of anywhere between $50 to $100. I couldn't afford a whole cross country paying any more than that when campgrounds were not available. But this one was especially bad. Someone must have taken a piss straight into the AC unit instead of the toilet, because as soon as I turned it on, the smell of urine overwhelmed the room. I hoped it would go away after a while, so I didn't complain, but it never did. I left the place in the morning carrying the "sweet" smell of urine inside my nostrils for quite some time. Oh, the places you spend the night!

Crossing beautiful spots along the Canalway.

Welcome to My Beloved Massachusetts

Ride 49 = Amsterdam, New York to Lanesborough, Massachusetts, 77.4 miles

Left the urine infested motel in Amsterdam after breakfast at a local joint that serves your very average breakfast menu, although it wasn't too bad, then went down the hills and back to the Canalway hoping for an easy day for a change.

I began with slow and easy pedaling as I do most days when I start my ride to allow my body to settle into the long and arduous task of cycling for many hours. At some point along the trail I met Ali, a lovely young girl taking a week off to ride part of the canal and experimenting for a possible cross country ride someday... way to go Ali. Start small, learn from your mistakes, then do it for real. Also, met four other touring cyclists on my last day at the Erie Canalway. A couple in their '60s doing the whole canal together and two young guys, brothers from Boston, who've been riding for five months across the country doing a brewery tour ... I meant to ask them how many hangovers they have had so far but they were in a hurry to get to the next stop - wonder why!! Talk about an efficient way to add and burn empty calories.

I exited the Canalway in Troy, before it actually ends in Albany so I could cut through Troy and go straight east into Massachusetts where I had planned to stay at a campground in Lanesborough for the night.

And so I hit the hills again. Haven't had that sort of climbing since... oh, since I left Wyoming to be honest. Eastern New York made me pay dearly for all the flat rides I had on the Erie Canal before I exited the state. Had some tough climbing to enter Massachusetts through Route 43 from Troy, but at some point I beheld a most welcome road sign "Welcome to Massachusetts," at the town of Hancock. Wow ... it's beginning to feel real. Thousands of revolutions on my crankset from the Pacific Ocean, and here I am, back in Massachusetts, a place that has given me a second nest in life. A few pictures later and it's time to make it real ... ride home.

Just as I thought I had enough of climbing for the day though, the road to my final destination happened to be called "Bradley Mountain Road" or something mountain road ... and it absolutely kicked me when I was down. It's end of August in the Berkshires, and just to be on the safe side before I took the one-mile gravel road into the campground, I thought better to call them first. The camp was closed for the season. Another wasted chance at camping.

Luckily just four miles down the road I found this lovely small motel for $55, the price being just a bit higher than a stay at KOA. The motel a walking distance from Matt Reilly's Irish Pub which sits by a beautiful lake in Lanesborough and serves Guinness and great dessert. How rewarding it is to find places with good vibe and nice people after a whole day of cycling. Had a sweet time eating and writing my notes before walking back to the motel to wash my clothes by hand again, as I did almost every night, and find a way to dry them in front of the AC.

I might make it!

Descent into Hill-Hell

Ride 50 = Lanesborough to Greenfield, Massachusetts, 49.3 miles

I planned to ride only 50 miles today. Although I expected some hills given that I had to cross the Green Mountains range in Western Massachusetts, nothing prepared me for what I went through today. Well, the Rockies at the other side of the country somewhat prepared me mentally. But I haven't had to climb a whole lot for the past few weeks. After all, they don't grow corn on mountains in Iowa, Illinois, Indiana and Ohio, states which I recently spent hundreds of miles.

After a belly-bulging breakfast in Lanesborough I climbed on my bicycle hoping to start slow due to my stuffed up state. It took me only 200 yards to start climbing in the route I had chosen. And so it went on for 50 miles. An infinite number of short but steep hills through beautiful farmland through the north of Massachusetts. Of course, you do go downhill at times, but that doesn't count! What you remember are the "ups" that bring you "down."

I haven't been this close to bonking in my entire trip. I'm sure it is quite as much psychological as it is physical. I wasn't expecting it to be this bad. And therein lays the challenge I guess. The weather was perfect. The Berkshires announces the fall ahead of every other place in Massachusetts. Despite of the sunny weather, I had to wear a jacket the entire day as the hills would make me sweat to the point of drenching my shirt, and the down hills with the increased wind would give me the chills.

Relying on Google maps to decide my route, even though it has a bicycle category, has never been the best choice. Yes, it usually brings me out of busy roads, which, in a sense, can be the most important factor if you want to have a level of peace of mind, but there's no category for "most bike friendly." You get what you get, often facing rough trails, gravel roads, and hilly routes that I wouldn't even want to ride my car through.

I failed to fill up my water bottles expecting to find plenty of little towns along the way, full of old fashioned general stores and even some Dunkin' Donuts for my iced coffees. But again, thanks to Google maps, you don't ride through busy areas, so I was probably meandering around main streets without even seeing them. By the time I entered the town of Greenfield I succeeded again at being badly hungry and thirsty. I didn't even bother looking around for a campground. The weather was turning cold already and my experience just fifty miles away, in Lanesborough, where the campground is closed for the season made me go straight into Rodeway Inn. It has been a failure, or I may say, a disheartening aspect of my trip that I had to stay in so many motels instead of camping. If I was driving a car it wouldn't be a problem to go in and out of the towns I stopped to find food and then return to campgrounds. But any five to ten miles to perform that task, or to access a campground location, can add to your misery at the end of a bicycle ride. This challenge is still attainable of course, but the truth is that most places don't have campgrounds nearby. It would be a completely different trip if I had the time to simply ride from camp to camp. I would need a lot more time than the fifty rides so far to cross the country. I would do it differently next time. Then again, who's talking about a next time?

I look forward to my last two rides. Tomorrow, Saturday, I plan to ride about 70 miles, then spend the night in some quaint town with nice, smiley good-looking people of good manners and intelligent conversation. Then Sunday, sleep late, have a starving-hyena breakfast, then ride another 60ish miles into Newburyport where some friends have warned me they will be waiting for me.

Rode through many beautiful places in Massachusetts I didn't know.

A Night of Mixed Feelings

Ride 51 = Greenfield to Leominster, Massachusetts, 63.2

Getting to Leominster was another day of an infinity of small hills. Massachusetts definitely wasn't built for cyclists. I'm avoiding any of the two or three main throughways to cross the state, so I had to weave my way around the north part of the state again, hitting every single hill that the state has to offer. It's the second to last ride and I am definitely not going to walk up any hill at this point, but the frequency to which they appear is a mighty motivation buster.

I had to get to Leominster somehow since I spent about two hours last night trying to figure out the best possible option for food and lodging and Leominster turned out to be my only solution. I didn't envision the last night at a motel again, but that's all I could find. I made several attempts to spend the night at an Airbnb around Leominster and the surrounding towns, but nothing came through.

A last lodging at a Days Inn before my final ride home somewhat chipped away the daily rugged and weathered character of my trip. Never mind the fact that it blew my budget even further. It fancied up a bit too much the image I had of myself at that point. Not that a Days Inn Motel is much to brag about either. But for a ragged, moldy and tired cyclist who was about to finish a coast-to-coast ride, I felt out of place among the other guests. Some who seemed to be attending fashion shows and weddings, and others perfectly shaved, tanned, adorned and perfumed with pinkish skin and toneless limbs getting ready for whatever it is that young people do these days for fun on a Saturday night.

Short of pitching my tent in the woods, there were no campgrounds available around here. Summer vibe ends fast in Massachusetts even when the weather hasn't yet announced the new season. But it was nice to take a good shower, wash my clothes, and walk downtown for a good dinner and a pint. Within the distance that took me to walk back from the restaurant to the motel, about four blocks only, I managed to get hungry again and for as long as I can remember I had dinner twice in one night. After just having had dinner and dessert I stopped at a fast food joint and bought a veggie burger and fries to go. I felt sick but finally full. I went to bed in a sort of mundane emotional state questioning if I should be a little more emotional, excited, sad. In fact, I felt quite bland asking myself what was wrong with me given this disconnect between the "magnitude" of my ride and my flat emotional state. Then I reminded myself that my feelings at that moment perhaps reflected the reality that all that was happening is the conclusion of a long *bicycle ride*. That's it. It shouldn't be looked as anything else. Nothing extraordinary accomplished. I rode a bicycle every day, ate a lot, spent more than I wanted, and didn't put in a single moment of "productive" time over the entire summer. So, why should I feel any different! Besides, is the last ride the beginning or the end?

Last Ride After All

Ride 52 = Leominster to Plum Island, 78 miles

Waking up numb and insipid, I sluggishly packed my stuff, put on some clean bike clothes, tossed away anything no longer necessary and got on my bicycle looking for an iced coffee.

At a coffee shop a few blocks from the motel, while I waited to place my order, a Spanish-speaking gentleman approached me to inquire about my loaded bicycle outside and what I was doing. My Spanish is not grammatically perfect, but I can communicate just fine. This nice senor told me about his love of bicycles and why he couldn't ride anymore. Listening to him it wasn't very clear to me that he couldn't. I asked further questions about his purported knee injuries and suggested that he should get back on a bicycle and start slow, build-up, the usual. We talked a little more; he got very excited about the idea of trying again. He then took a twenty dollar bill out of his pocket and offered it to me, because, as he put it, "people should be supporting you for doing this." I obviously thanked him for the offer and said I could not accept it. He wouldn't have it. He said I had just inspired him to exercise again. Fearing that we were making a bit of a scene by now - him putting money in my hand and me returning it - I just took the bill, gave him a big hug and left.

It was the culmination of a long string of good human beings I had the good fortune of meeting throughout my trip. So many gentle characters whom through the power of a smile, the offer of food and water, prayer, good wishes, good vibes, hugs and advice, have further strengthened my conviction that people are better than we are told. The vast majority are.

I left the coffee shop with a smile tucked in my chest. I knew I had over seventy miles to ride today before reaching Newburyport, but I wasn't in a hurry at all. Today, I would not be carrying my bicycle and bags; my bicycle would carry me. At whatever pace Scarlet and the roads allow me.

I plugged in my destination on Google maps without any concern and allowed it to take me where it wanted. Which was very much like the previous days in Massachusetts. A bit flatter, but a festival of zig-zagging, weaving and turning through back roads that always seemed to be leading nowhere. However, I got to know a wealth of beautiful parts of the state that I never knew existed. At some point, Google made me cross into Southern New Hampshire, making it the fourteenth state I would hit in my cross country trip.

Back into Massachusetts, I ended up crossing right through Methuen just as a sort of intense "free-form" Spanish parade or fiesta was taking over the streets with loud speakers, boastful youth and dangerous double-parking that pretty much turned me into a tiny little cycling bug, which could be squished at any moment without any second thoughts.

I had one larger city to ride through, Lawrence, also a poorly chosen route by google, especially as it put me through downtown, battling roads chaotic and damaged enough for cars, never mind bicycles. But I made it through, and soon road signs began to display names of familiar towns and villages I could recall having been through one time or another in the past few years.

It is needless to state at this point my love of music. I go out of my way to search for songs, classical and jazz pieces, international artists, new talented composers and bands to fulfill my unquenchable thirst for the largest possible variety of great music that I can find. I don't want to miss anything!

Such was the case with one composition by American flugelhorn player Chuck Mangione titled, "I've Never Missed Someone Before." I've been in love with that song since my early 20s. The piece starts with a sweet simple line played solo on piano then repeated again on flute, then guitar. That sort of simplicity that reaches the heights of Olympus without any pretentious exuberance. After the guitar, comes Mangione with his mellow, perfect, rich flugelhorn playing along with the bass. The beautiful line is repeated a few more times before the song veers toward a variation on the theme, and the crescendo and improvising begins with so much taste it makes you want to be in that moment forever.

On my handlebar speaker the music was on, and softly, the first piano notes began to sound off that beautiful melody: "I've Never Missed Someone Before." I'm coming home. I'm about to hit the other edge of America, right where Pietra is buried under a bed of flowers in my yard. I'm reaching the end of a trip that, honestly, I wasn't quite sure I could pull off, nor if I would finish in one piece! It dawned on me for the first time that something deep inside my chest could take the best of my emotional control today and carry me to a place where an overwhelming joy breaks you in half.

I rode the 9 minutes and 37 seconds of that song not wanting it to ever end. And by the end of it, the ground beneath my tires had the scent of many former rides. I began to feel at home. The roads, the towns, the character of New England embedded in the streets I knew. And that thing growing inside my chest.

Two blocks away from the corner of Route 113 and Bachelor Street in Newbury, my excitement grew exponentially. I knew that some of the master swimmers I coach, who are now such dear friends to me would be on their bikes waiting to join me for the last few miles.

Bob, Lynette, Pam, and the wonderful Amanda, who for days had kept track of my progress and whereabouts to make sure that I would be on my predicted time of arrival, were there to greet me.

After 52 rides and more than 3,800 miles I pressed down on my pedals toward the cheering faces of my friends who embraced me with the kindest smiles one could receive.

But I still had about 10 miles to go before dipping my front wheel in the Atlantic Ocean at Plum Island. I began to think I was actually going to finish this ride after all. I recalled looking at the ocean on the shores of Fort Stevens in Oregon and thinking that Plum Island would be such an impossible goal to reach.

We all rode together through Newburyport and finally into the main road leading to Plum Island. More cyclists were waiting for me and lined up behind my bicycle for the final two miles. They naturally allowed me to take the lead. I guess I unconsciously took the lead feeling anxious to finish.

About half mile away from the ocean I see a large crowd gathering at a bar at the entrance of Plum Island. My vision gets fuzzy. My eyes are covered with that *liquid substance* that emanates from inside of you when your emotions take over your existence.

Another couple of hundred yards and I'm riding past a large cheering crowd clapping and screaming. One block from the ocean now. I'm approaching the entrance to the beach and a large banner made by my friends and swimmers is being held high for me to ride under, with the words "Congrats Ron" written on it. I'm speechless. I'm smiling, I see so many faces, but my eyes are covered with tears. I go under the banner, dismount, and begin to push my bicycle over deep sand. It's about twenty yards now till I feel the water. I see and hear everyone around me but I'm so overwhelmed with emotion that my body moves *alone* in time and space for those last yards. I see someone taking lots of pictures walking along with me.

Amanda had arranged everything. The large group of friends, the banner, and the local newspaper's photographer to report on my arrival. I'm not sure if I expressed my gratitude as much as I felt Amanda, but if you're ever reading this, know that you made that day so much more special to me. I'll be forever grateful to you for my memorable welcome and to your husband for the beautiful pictures.

One more step. And my bicycle shoes and front wheel are in. 3,850 miles later I step into the Atlantic. I'm surrounded by people I love. I'm confused. I look around but I don't acknowledge anybody's faces. I'm trying to hold it together. I know there's something else I should do, so I turn around and ask someone to hold Scarlet.

Making sure that all my pockets are empty I dive into the ocean and pump both fists up. My friends clap and cheer again. I walk back toward my bicycle, bend over it, resting my forehead over my seat ... and unhinge... I sob like a child.

In an effort to congratulate me, a well-intentioned stranger hands me a ... Bud Light!! Oh well!

A quarter of a mile from the Atlantic. Feeling the love!

Amanda pumping her fist to cheer me on and to make sure I don't quit!

My friends and awesome swimmers, Cal and Dan, welcoming me in the right theme!

Craig and Claire. What can I say! What a welcome.

Overwhelmed!

THE END

Epilogue

It has been six months since I completed my cross-country ride. I've finally finished editing the account of each ride, chosen the pictures for the book, received the final proofread from my friend and swimmer Jim Murphy, a professional writer, and now I'm a few days away from publishing it.

But the ride hasn't left my mind one single day. The overall feeling hasn't changed either. I still don't see the completion of it as anything grand. Sure my kindergarten students think I've crossed the entire world in just a few days... but I guess I can indulge myself in a little ego-boosting from tiny admirers. I'm obviously proud of myself for having done it, at my age especially, but, most of all, I just feel a sense of joy for the opportunity that life presented me. I'm *grateful* for having been out there on my bicycle getting to know "*so many roads*."

It didn't take me long at all to begin thinking "what's next?" and a week-long group ride around New England named "New England Ride-Around" was born. Several swimmers from the masters team I coach are helping me organize this event, and we intend to make it an annual ride as soon as we can officially incorporate our club. But regardless, the truth is that I have caught the bug. I now recognize like never before the allure of the road, especially from the top of a bike seat. If before I was an avid cyclist going on area rides, now I want to be out there in the world. I don't know exactly how or if I will engage in such long rides again, but the desire is firmly established in my heart now.

Because *my legs cranked on!* Luckily!

As I stepped out of the Atlantic Ocean, on the day of my arrival, all my friends surrounded me in expectation of what I was going to say. I could tell they wanted me to put that moment in words. The stage was perfectly set for me to say something "grand." But all I could come up with was "we can all do much more than we think we can." Nothing especial. In those milliseconds before your mouth spews and reveals the emptiness of your brain, I knew I was going to make a complete fool out of myself. However, what came out was the sum of my surprise that my legs kept me going when my mind couldn't any further.

I had no real sense of what to expect before I embarked on this cross-country ride in relation to the capacity of my body to actually go through the challenge of dozens and dozens of miles per day, with no days off. Often, at the end of each day's ride I would worry about the next day. It wasn't clear to me at all that my body could do it again the day after. What if that little pain I'm feeling turns out to be a serious injury? What if the accumulation of thousands of circular motions upon my hip and knee joints day after day would just cause it to snap, or seize, or hurt beyond my ability to withstand? I wish I didn't have those thoughts. Perhaps a younger version of me wouldn't.

I recall one particular day in the middle of a ride when one of these thoughts came to my head, and sure enough, just a few minutes later the quadriceps on my right leg started to hurt. A sharp, piercing pain. I couldn't believe it. Did my brain cause it to hurt? Did my brain anticipate the pain in order to prepare my body for it? Was it just psychosomatic? The fact is the pain was real, and for the rest of the day I struggled to press on the pedal due to a combination of muscle pain and weakness coming from that leg. And yet, next day I was fine. Felt it again, a little, midway through the day, but nothing that would prevent me from keep on rolling. There were many, many other instances of discerning aches, soreness, discomforts, tingles and tenderness that begged for the same good fortune. At the end, it came down to pure luck I think.

But I also credit the ability to ride every day to a few factors. First, I was riding alone, so I could set the pace according to what my body was telling me at each moment. I started every morning at a slow pace and gave my body plenty of time to adjust. Second, I was very diligent in regards to stretching before and after each ride, especially at the end. In the morning, I would try to feel my muscles somewhat loose before hopping on my bicycle. At night, I stretched to the limit of each joint and held it for several seconds, or until reaching that feeling of relaxation that only deep stretching begets. Also, I never neglected hydration. Especially by keeping my bottles full of iced water as often as possible thanks to those life-saving, self-serving soda machines one finds at general stores and fast food places, where the ice and water is often free of charge. Alright, the nurturing pints at night might have something to do with it as well.

Regardless of any single factor, looking back I recollect the sense of joy and relief that my legs were actually able to carry me to my destination each day.

And then there's Luna!

Luna is a recently adopted amazingly sweet five-year-old feline who is doing her best right now to rescue a marriage.

Luna!

Made in the USA
Middletown, DE
13 August 2018